MORRIS VENDEN

LOVE GOD

AND DO AS

YOU PLEASE

A New Look at the Old Rules

Pacific Press Publishing Association
Boise, Idaho
Oshawa, Ontario, Canada

The author assumes full responsibility for all quotations cited in this book.

Edited by Jerry D. Thomas
Designed by Tim Larson
Cover design by Tim Larson
Typeset in 10/12 Century Schoolbook

Library of Congress Cataloging-in-Publication Data:
    Venden, Morris L.
    Love God and do as you please: a new look at the old rules
/ Morris Venden.
        p.   cm.
    ISBN 0-8163-1089-0
    1.   Christian   ethics—Seventh-day   Adventist   authors.
I. Title.
BJ1012.V43.1992   91-39698
241'.046732—dc20   CIP

92 93 94 95 96 • 5 4 3 2 1

Contents

Introduction

Perhaps you will consider the title to this book a shocker. Undoubtedly, the immature will misunderstand it. Some will misuse it as an excuse for license and loose living. Some will use it as a reason for criticizing the author. But if they read the book, they might get the right message.

Mature Christians can do as they please because what they please to do also pleases God. Listen to the good news in better words than mine.

If we consent, He [God] will so identify Himself with our thoughts and aims, so blend our hearts and minds into conformity to His will, that when obeying Him we shall be but carrying out our own impulses (*The Desire of Ages*, p. 668).

If we abide in Christ, if the love of God dwells in us, our feelings, our thoughts, our purposes, our actions, will be in harmony with the will of God (*Steps to Christ*, p. 61).

Looking unto Jesus we obtain brighter and more distinct views of God, and by beholding we become changed. Goodness, love for our fellow men, becomes our natural instinct (*Christ's Object Lessons*, p. 355).

When we submit ourselves to Christ, the heart is united with His heart, the will is merged in His will, the mind becomes one with His mind, the thoughts are brought into captivity to Him; we live His life. This is what it means to be clothed with the garments of His righteousness (Ibid., p. 312).

Need we say more?

One

True or False Obedience

Remember the Mud Puddle Kid? In the story, from Ken McFarland's *Gospel Showdown*, God is the mother, and you and I are Mud Puddle Kids.

Halfway through his nightly recital of the world's hang-ups, the benign anchorman suddenly disappeared, replaced momentarily by that commercial starring the Mud Puddle Kid.

Draped across various items of living-room furniture out there in front of the box were the Three Watchers.

"That poor Kid's mother really has a problem," Number One observed, as, up on the screen, The Kid stomped gleefully through several large mud puddles. "She probably had him all ready to go to a party, and now look at him with that yucky mud all over his clothes."

"Oh, but there's Good News!" enthused Number Two excitedly. "Just watch now," he added, pointing to the screen, "and you'll see that his mom is going to take all those dirty clothes and wash them in Mud-B-Gone detergent. That will solve everything!"

"If you've watched this commercial before, then you ought to know that that doesn't solve everything," retorted Number One. "Just keep watching."

They did, and sure enough, The Kid, sporting freshly laundered clothes, charged back outside to the nearest puddle. As he splattered himself with muddy goo, his mom shook her head and sighed as she tried to look thankful for her box of Mud-B-Gone.

"There, you see," Number One continued. "What good does it do for her to clean her Kid up if he goes right back out and jumps in the mud? I'll tell you what the real Good News is. It's when Mom not only can clean The Kid up, but can also take away his desire to play in mud puddles—maybe even make him hate mud."

Number Three hadn't said anything so far, but he'd been thinking, and now he was ready with his dime's worth. "I think both of you may have a point," he began, "but even if Mom can clean up The Kid and then make him hate mud puddles, it seems to me that the problem can never be fully solved until someone takes the mud puddles themselves away. To me, that would really be Good News."

Well, it pains me to say it, but the Three Watchers became so upset with one another over what constituted the Good News, or the Gospel, that they decided to have a showdown. They stepped out into the street and started slinging mud at one another.

The last I saw them, they still hadn't figured out that they had all three seen just a part of the Good News—and that it takes all three parts to really solve The Kid's problem.

But, as Walter Cronkite used to say, "That's the way it is."[1]

I am glad that God has made provision to wash us clean by His grace and forgive our sins. This is the first part of solving our problem.

As for the second part, are we glad that God has made provision to keep us out of the mud puddles? Or would we rather splash ourselves with muddy goo? And here comes the crucial question: Do we stay out of the mud just to please Mother? Or do we stay out of the mud because we *want* to stay out of mud, because we don't like mud? Can we say we even hate mud?

Of course, we all look forward to the third part, the day when there will be no mud puddles, either in Iraq or Bangladesh or China or the United States. When Jesus returns, all mud puddles will dry up.

Let's consider that second part—staying out of the mud. You cannot get into the great theme of righteousness by faith without getting into the topic of obedience. But, in the past, many people have had the idea that faith is somehow against obedience, that if you're going to be friendly to faith, you have to be unfriendly to obedience. And if you're going to be friendly to obedience, then, by all means, you can't be friendly to faith. Some have used faith as a banner to march under as an escape from obedience. "Oh, that doesn't matter anymore," they say. "All you have to do is have faith." Forgotten are the words of Scripture that say you can never separate faith and obedience. They always, always, go together. Obedience is the fruit of faith. You can't separate apples from healthy apple trees. You can't have one without the other, and if you have one, you're going to have the other.

According to Scripture, obedience is clearly important. Learn from the wise man, Solomon, who wasn't so wise after all. He had to learn by his own mistakes. After he had experienced 700 wives and 300 concubines, and an entire lifetime, he finally discovered that "all is vanity" (Ecclesiastes 12:8). Then he said, "Let us hear the conclusion of the whole matter . . ." Here, a man who is old enough to die before he knows enough to live, says, Come now, let's get down to the nitty-gritty. This is the conclusion of the whole matter: "Fear God, and keep his commandments: for this is the whole *duty* of man" (verse 13, emphasis supplied).

Here we have a major clue as to one of Solomon's problems. Anyone who thinks that keeping God's commandments is a *duty* is off to the wrong start. Maybe he wasn't quite smart enough to realize, even at that time of his life, that something more is involved in obedience than duty. If the only reason I obey is because of duty, then my religion is worth nothing.

There are those who profess to serve God, while they rely upon their own efforts to obey His law, to form a right character, and secure salvation. Their hearts are not moved by any deep sense of love of Christ, but they seek to perform the *duties* of the Christian life as that which God requires of them in order to gain heaven. Such religion is worth nothing (*Steps to Christ*, emphasis supplied).

"But," someone says, "won't such religion eventually lead me to Christ?" No, "such religion is worth nothing." And yet many of us have grown up that way. In fact, we carry it over into the church from childhood. We have had instruction from the family experts—and even from the inspired pen—that we should train our young people, our boys and girls, in proper habits and the right kind of obedience. Teach them to obey. Teach them to obey from duty. Teach them to obey because Father and Mother said so, because it's the right thing to do. And we like to quote statements like, "Be as true to duty as the needle to the pole" (*Education*, p. 57).

As we have continued to emphasize this approach, we have developed a whole subculture of people who think of obedience in terms of duty. I would like to suggest that obedience that is nothing more than duty is false obedience, always false obedience.

Let's take a look at the difference between true obedience and false obedience. Here is a remarkable and almost revolutionary quotation:

All *true* obedience comes from the heart. It was heart work with Christ. And if we consent, He will so identify Himself with our thoughts and aims, so blend our hearts

10

and minds into conformity to His will, that when obeying Him we shall be but carrying out our own impulses. The will, refined and sanctified, will find its highest delight in doing His service. When we know God as it is our privilege to know Him, our life will be a life of continual obedience. Through an appreciation of the character of Christ, through communion with God, sin will become hateful to us (*The Desire of Ages,* p. 668, emphasis supplied).

The Scripture says of Jesus, our example, "I delight to do thy will, O my God: yea, thy law is within my heart" (Psalm 40:8), and "He loved righteousness and hated 'mud puddles.'" So all genuine, true obedience—the kind that Jesus had—springs naturally from within, from the heart, the thoughts, the purposes, the motives transformed by grace. Any obedience that does not come from that source is false obedience. Which means that many of us have been victims of and have experienced a lot of false obedience.

Here is the usual brand of false obedience, dressed up a little bit and made to look good by bringing Jesus into the picture: "You should stay out of the mud because you love Jesus." "OK. Well, I love Jesus, so I guess I have to stay out of the mud." (This is a form of staying out of the mud in order to please Mother.)

Another version is not quite as subtle but perhaps just as bad—if we don't obey, we crucify Jesus anew.

"Look at the spikes that you drive through His hands and feet!" They say, "Every time you get in the mud, another spike goes into Jesus. You're going to hurt Him."

People have said to me, "I really can't handle this kind of guilt approach." And I have to agree. In the first place, is Jesus the kind of being who is going to sit around getting His feelings hurt every time we fall or fail? And what kind of a guilt trip does this concept lay on people, "You drove another nail!"?

This approach, so common in many circles, this trying to stay out of the mud in order to please Him or in order not to hurt Him or drive another nail, can also lead to discourage-

11

ment and to backsliding. Sooner or later people will scrap that kind of thing. We have to offer something better than this *duty* obedience, this false obedience, this guilt-ridden obedience. If we don't, we will join the ranks of those who say, "Oh, c'mon, let's just forget the whole business and hang with faith. Faith is all that counts. Forget about obedience. Don't talk about it."

I'm thankful for a Bible that talks about something better.

This brings us to the question, Is it possible for us to obey in the first place? One mentality says: "Watch out! You're getting too idealistic, and you're going to get into perfectionism. Don't talk about staying out of the mud. We can't. We're just weak human beings, and we'll continue to wade through the mud until Jesus comes. That's why we can be so thankful for Mud-B-Gone [justification]. So, let's take our refuge in Mud-B-Gone."

Well, it's true that you can find passages in Scriptures that *seem* to talk this way. Romans, written by someone who was pretty well-known on this subject, says this in chapter 7, verses 18 through 23:

> I know that in me (that is, in my flesh) dwelleth no good thing: for to will is present with me; but how to perform that which is good I find not. For the good that I would I do not: but the evil which I would not, that I do. . . . I delight in the law of God after the inward man [evidently there is something there that he likes about it]: but I see another law in my members, warring against the law of my mind, and bringing me into captivity to the law of sin which is in my members.

> To will is present with me but how to perform that which is good I find not.

Now this was written by a man who, in Philippians 3, tells how he was a blameless sinner before he came to Christ. So he was pretty good at performance. But when it came to the deeper life, looking at the heart and the motives, the apostle Paul realized that he was in a wretched condition. Then does that mean that it is not possible to obey?

In the days of Christ, the religious people developed a system of purely external obedience based on their past history. You see, Moses and his successors stood in front of the people and said, "Obey and live, disobey and die. If you obey you'll be blessed; if you disobey you'll be cursed." And they experienced some strong evidence supporting this principle. In fact, if you go through the Old Testament record, it's pretty hard to miss the point that obedience brings God's blessing, and disobedience brings God's cursing. Do you mean that God brings cursing? Well, that's the way it reads. Have you checked it out lately?

Let's take a look at the bad news about disobedience. "If they obey not, they shall perish by the sword, and they shall die without knowledge" (Job 36:12). Well, that's from one of Job's friends. We're not too sure about him.

Wait a minute! Jeremiah says, "If they will not obey, I will utterly pluck up and destroy that nation, saith the Lord" (Jeremiah 12:17). Who is going to do it? Is the Lord going to turn them over to the devil to bring the curse? No, "*I* will utterly pluck up and destroy that nation." What about 2 Thessalonians 1, verses 7 and 8? "The Lord Jesus shall be revealed from heaven with his mighty angels, in flaming fire taking vengeance on them that know not God, and that obey not the gospel of our Lord Jesus Christ." The punishment is not turned over to the devil. God and the devil are not business associates and good partners. The Bible is clear that blessings come with obedience, and lack of blessings comes with disobedience.

Did the church in the days of Christ understand this principle? See for yourself: "Whatsoever we ask, we receive of him, because we keep his commandments, and do those things that are pleasing in his sight" (1 John 3:22). How can you miss the message that blessings come with obedience? Answered prayers for special favors come with obedience. We receive them because we keep His commandments and do His works. Oh, someone says, that sounds like salvation by works. No, this is not talking about salvation; it's talking about blessings.

And there is a big difference between obeying to be saved in heaven and obeying and receiving His blessings.

A blind man (see John 9) was hauled in before the Jewish leaders. They tried to get him to tell where he'd come from and who had healed him. The religious leaders were after Jesus. The blind man's own family had become frightened and left him. Finally, this lone blind man stood before these leaders, teaching them! He said in verse 31, "Now we know that *God heareth not sinners*: but if any man be a worshipper of God, and doeth his will, him he heareth" (emphasis supplied). What is he basing this on? He's basing this on the clear Old Testament record: Blessings come with obedience; lack of blessings comes with disobedience. This principle shows up again and again in Scripture. Salvation by works? No. We're not talking about salvation.

Well, when those people heard about the warnings against disobedience and the appeal to obedience, they said, "We'd better obey so we can get the blessing." So we have a whole nation of people who were constantly trying to obey in order to get the blessing. That was their motive. But the only thing they could produce was outward obedience.

Outward obedience has never deceived God, although it has deceived many people. Strong-willed people can, and often have, faked it on the outside. And it is possible to establish entire churches on that basis, if our primary focus, as the basis of our Christian life, is on behavior. But Jesus said, unless your righteousness exceeds that of the scribes and the Pharisees, unless it's true, inward obedience, there's no way you can enter into the kingdom of heaven.

One year at Christmastime, when I was a child, my father and I were looking in a store downtown when I saw a fire engine. It was a big fire engine with a siren and a light. It even moved by its own power. I desperately wanted that fire engine! Then I remembered some children's Christmas songs: "You better watch out, you better not cry, you better not pout," and, "Just before Christmas I am as good as I can be." So I decided to be as good as I could be in order to get the fire engine. Good idea? Well, I was as good as I could be, but I

14

didn't get the fire engine. And guess what I did then? I wasn't interested in being good anymore. In fact, I was interested in being bad because I didn't get the fire engine. Did I do the right thing? Or did I do the normal thing?

That kind of reasoning was a major problem in the days of Christ. People wanted the blessings, but they didn't want the Lord. I want my prayers to be heard when trouble comes, but I am not really interested in the One to whom I am praying.

And so we come to this question: Is it really possible to produce something more than simply outward obedience? This brings us to Romans 8:3, 4, which clearly says this:

> What the law could not do, in that it was weak through the flesh [There is no way that you or I or the apostle Paul can keep the commandments in our own strength. We are weak through the flesh], God sending his own Son in the likeness of sinful flesh, and for sin, condemned sin in the flesh: that the righteousness of the law might be fulfilled in us, who walk not after the flesh, but after the Spirit.

Now, some people like to read it this way: "That the righteousness of the law might be fulfilled *for* us in Jesus' life. He becomes my substitute obedience because I can't obey. All I can do is fall and fail and sin. So He becomes my substitute in that department as well." No, that's not the way the Bible reads. "That the righteousness of the law might be fulfilled *in us*, who walk not after the flesh, but after the Spirit." Or in other words, we who are not trying to obey in our own power but are seeking the Spirit of God, as Jesus did. We who are trying to work from the inside out instead of simply outside duty and coercion for the purpose of getting the blessing. This is the principle of true obedience—the only kind there is.

I'd like to remind you that many of us have wasted a lot of time and effort trying to obey. And the only thing we ever produced was false obedience. Well, should we forget that? No, because false obedience is worthwhile in this world. If I feel like shooting you, and I don't do it, there are going to be some real benefits. One of them would be to you, and the other one would be to me. If I feel like stealing something, and I grit my teeth and get my backbone up and I don't steal it, then there are going to be some real benefits.

Morality, which is the worldly word for outward obedience, is worthwhile. It counts in this world. It keeps you out of jail. It keeps you from getting traffic tickets. It keeps your reputation good. Nobody is against morality. Let's have all the morality we can have. But morality never has been obedience, and it isn't obedience today. Outward duty, outward performance, is not real obedience. But we've done a lot of it. I've done a lot of it. Strong people can obey outwardly, but weak people can't. And that's why false obedience is so tricky. Because if behavior is our emphasis, then we can fill the church with strong people and leave weak people out in the cold.

Then Jesus came along and showed an entirely different kind of obedience—a kind that came from above Him, rather than from His own self-generated efforts. This is the beauty of Jesus' life. He came to live life as we have to live it. Not as a God, but as a human being. He could have depended upon Himself for all kinds of power. But He didn't. And the power we see demonstrated in His life, in terms of His mighty works and His miracles—including His power for obedience—came from above Him, not from within Him. And this power can come for us, but only as we sing the song that nobody means.

Elder Richards used to say, "Let's sing the song that nobody means. 'Have thine own way, Lord. Have thine own way! Thou art the Potter; I am the clay.' " That's scary. We don't like the idea of surrendering to the Lord. It might change our lifestyle. It might spoil our fun. It might make us really obedient, and maybe that would be boring.

But that's what the apostle Paul talks about. Since the law could not make us obedient because there's no power in the law (it is weak through my flesh) God sent His own Son and showed us an example of obedience that comes from above. That's the real kind of obedience, from the heart, from love. And then we are told that we can live the kind of life that Jesus lived. Oh, really? Yes!

16

One time someone asked me, "Can anyone live without sinning?" I replied that I would like to change the question. For there was One who lived life in this world without sinning. So the question should be restated, Can Jesus live His life in me? That's the question. Apart from Jesus, can anyone live a life without sinning? No. Apart from Jesus, can anyone live an obedient life? No. All that we can produce is false. But is it possible for Jesus to live His life in me?

As we consider this question, we need to read one of the most beautiful passages in all Scripture concerning this very point, Hebrews 13:20, 21.

Now the God of peace, that brought again from the dead our Lord Jesus, that great shepherd of the sheep, through the blood of the everlasting covenant, make you perfect in every good work to do his will, working *in you that which is well pleasing in his sight,* through Jesus Christ (emphasis supplied).

The method and the goal and the possibility are all listed here. Make you perfect. How perfect? In every good work. What does that mean? To do His will, *by working in you.*

First Thessalonians 5:23 and 24 says, "The very God of peace sanctify you wholly; and I pray God your whole spirit and soul and body be preserved blameless unto the coming of our Lord Jesus Christ. Faithful is he that calleth you, *who also will do it"* (emphasis supplied). *He* will do it. And Philippians 2:13 says, "It is God which worketh in you both to will and to do of his good pleasure." And Galatians 2:20 says, "I am crucified with Christ: nevertheless I live; yet not I, but Christ liveth in me: and the life which I now live in the flesh I live by the faith of the Son of God, who loved me, and gave himself for me."

The Bible does not talk about merely falling and failing and producing false obedience until Jesus comes. This Bible talks about being more than conquerors through Him. Do you believe that? Then, away with the idea that obedience is just too complicated, too hard. Away with the idea that obedience is impossible, so we'll just have to march under the banner of

17

faith. The Bible doesn't teach that all we can do is fall and fail until He comes. No, the Bible doesn't talk that way at all. It promises blessing for obedience. It promises lack of blessing for disobedience. It tells us that *we* cannot obey, but *He* can, and He can live His life in us.

I am painfully aware how quiet people get when we talk about obedience. I've seen it happen again and again in different parts of the country. Someone gets up and talks about faith and grace and the cross and Jesus—how He died for our sins and how He washes away our sins—and everybody says, "Praise the Lord, Hallelujah." Someone talks about obedience and overcoming and power, and everyone gets quiet—and so do I. Because I remember how I blew it yesterday. And I'll probably fall again and fail tomorrow. That's why I get quiet. What then do we do? Simply this; if we keep in touch with Jesus, the work that He has begun He will carry forward to the day of His return.

False obedience is like the *sp sp sp sp sp* of the diesel engine on the tugboat in the harbor. You have to come from a harbor town to appreciate this parable. I have been somewhere near the harbor a time or two and heard the tugboats starting up in the morning. They begin with *boom boom, sp sp, sp, boom, sp, sp sp, boom, boom, sp sp sp, boom, boom*. Little by little, you get the impression that something is trying to get going. The *boom booms* would be the true obedience, and the *sp sp sp* would be the false obedience. And the whole idea with this tugboat, out there in the harbor, is for the engine to continue to warm up until it goes *boom boom boom boom boom* all the time.

My life and your life and the life of anyone who is trying to produce obedience and has grappled with this problem is very much like that engine trying to get going. We hit on only one cylinder to begin with, but eight are available. Little by little, as we grow in Christ, we begin to understand more and more what it means to have genuine obedience.

Part of my plea here is for us to stop calling false obedience real. Let's stop giving our boys and girls the idea that false obedience is the real thing. Let's remind them that there is something far better available. Let's keep teaching our young people habits of obedience and right living just as much as we can, if just to keep them out of jail long enough to start hitting on all eight cylinders someday. But, let's not give them the impression that what is really false is the real thing, because, sooner or later, they'll walk away from the fake experience. Thousands of people, young and old alike, have already walked away from that.

Someone handed me this parable, in which Hawaii represents obedience and perfection: The town of Remnant, California, was officially organized in 1863. However, the earliest settlers began to gather in that location around 1844. People who lived in Remnant were different in many ways from the rest of the world. But they had one outstanding teaching. The people of Remnant believed that everyone should move to Hawaii. (Now remember, Hawaii represents obedience.) From the first they had been sure that the sooner folks made it to Hawaii, the sooner they would make it to heaven. But there was one extremely embarrassing fact that they could not escape. They didn't live in Hawaii. Hawaii seemed to be a long way off. Almost as far away as heaven itself. And while a few of them claimed to have been to Hawaii, nobody believed that they really had. There was a common saying in Remnant: If you say you've been to Hawaii, that is sure proof you've never been there.

Most of the people in Remnant believed that if you worked as hard as you could for your entire lifetime, maybe you'd be able to spend one day in Hawaii just before you died. And few would manage even that. Although the population of Remnant numbered several million, most accepted the fact that if a hundred and forty-four thousand of them made it to Hawaii, even for a short time, that would be about the best that could be expected.

For a number of years, there was one commonly accepted method for trying to reach Hawaii. You went out to the beach, got into the water, and started swimming. Swimming lessons were popular in Remnant, as you might imagine. Children were expected to learn to swim almost before they learned to walk. There were swimming schools and swimming seminars and five-day swimming clinics offered regularly. Anyone who was a citizen in good and regular standing was expected to learn to swim. Newcomers to town were warned that it might take some time before they could swim well enough to actually reach Hawaii, but they were expected to begin swimming right away. All were encouraged by the thought that if they would do their part and try hard every day, sooner or later they would succeed in making it to Hawaii.

Some became so discouraged with trying and failing, trying and failing, that they left town. Others died in their attempts. But most everybody kept trying to swim to Hawaii until, one day, the inevitable happened.

A swimmer had just been forced to turn back toward shore, failing once again to make it to Hawaii, when he had what seemed to be a flash of insight. As soon as he got his breath, he began going up and down the beach and all around town asking, "Who says we have to live in Hawaii anyway? Do you realize how long we've been trying to make it to Hawaii? Can you name even one person who has ever made it?" Before long, he gathered quite a following, all asking the same question. And they came to the same conclusion. It is not necessary to go to Hawaii.

And they began to spread their good news far and near. Some people gladly accepted this new idea. Others fought against it. For a time, everyone in Remnant seemed to be discussing the new theology, the idea that even if they kept on trying to reach Hawaii, right up until they were taken to heaven, nobody would ever even come close. But, the good news claimed, it didn't matter.

So, now there were two groups, the one group still insisting that it was necessary to live in Hawaii, and the other group was sure that it was not. (But interestingly enough, both groups still went regularly to the beach to practice their swimming.)

Then came news of a third option. It sounded weird. It bypassed the beach entirely. The third option was to get acquainted with the airplane pilot and place yourself in His hands. Then you depend on Him to get you to Hawaii. And when you get on board the plane with the Pilot in control, all you have to do is rest. It is His business to get you to Hawaii.

It seemed difficult to understand at first. The questions came thick and fast. So what do you do? Do you wave your arms? Do you kick your feet? Do you jog up and down the aisle of the plane? When so many had failed to reach Hawaii in spite of the tremendous struggles and backbreaking work, how could anyone expect to reach that tropical paradise by resting? It sounded pleasant, but surely it was only a myth. Hawaii had always meant effort, lots of effort. Surely there must be some misunderstanding.

Some tried to explain that there was effort involved in getting acquainted with the Pilot, in boarding the plane, and even in the resting itself. But it didn't sound like real effort at all, not compared to what had been going on down at the beach.

The discussions about the third option went something like this: "Our part is to rest and to continue to place ourselves under the control of the Pilot."

Someone would look puzzled and ask, "Do you mean we don't have to go to Hawaii after all?"

"Yes, it is essential to go to Hawaii."

"Well, then we'd better get back down to the beach and stop standing around talking about it."

"No, we will never reach Hawaii by swimming for it."

"Then it is impossible to go to Hawaii."

"You mean we don't have to go?"

"Yes, we do. Living in Hawaii is possible. It is important. It is necessary."

"Then we'd better start swimming."

"No, no, no, we'd better head for the airport."

Little by little, here and there, people began to get the message. And as they did, they began to make regular trips to Hawaii. It was true that they didn't talk about going there. They talked about the Pilot and the airplane and the rest that was offered. As they continued to share and reach out to the tired swimmers, the good news began to spread.

21

What happened then? Well, some who had been the best swimmers and had ventured the farthest out into the cold waters of the Pacific Ocean were insulted. They were heard to say, "If they're letting people get to Hawaii by depending on someone else to take them there, then I don't want to go anyway." So they left the water and the beach and the town and moved to Las Vegas.

But some of the worst swimmers, who had barely managed to stay afloat, were among the first ones to rush to the airport and board the plane with the Pilot. Before too long, everyone had gone one way or the other. In the end, the beach was empty. Nobody went swimming anymore.

---

1. Ken McFarland, *Gospel Showdown* (Boise, Idaho: Pacific Press Publishing Association, 1981).

Chapter
Two

Loving the Law

Pacific Union College has its own Indianapolis 500 speedway. It's the eight miles from the top of Howell Mountain into the valley below. The students there face an almost uncontrollable urge to see how fast they can make it up and down that mountain in their Porsches and Corvettes. It used to bring the used-car-lot personality out of me. My family called it my used-car-lot personality when I chased a student up or down the mountain.

One day as I was driving down the mountain, I saw one of the students, who was burning the road, run a little old white-haired lady into the ditch. I was angry! I felt that I was justifiably angry. And I didn't know what to do, because he was instantly far ahead of me and out of sight. But when I came down to the bottom of the mountain and saw him sitting by the side of the road in front of a black car with white sides and lights on top, I said, "Oh, how love I the law. It is my meditation all the day."

How long has it been since you said, "Oh, how love I the

law. It is my meditation all the day"? Somewhere along the line we've gotten the idea that the law of God is unfriendly to faith; that the law of God is unfriendly to Jesus; that it is unfriendly to the great theme of salvation through faith in Christ alone. But, I'd like to remind you that the path to the Promised Land goes past Mount Sinai. And Mount Sinai leads to Calvary. So, we have some important things to consider about the law of God.

When we take a look at the different topics surrounding the teaching of salvation through faith in Christ alone, sooner or later we come face to face with obedience to the law of God. Do you consider it friendly or unfriendly? What is the purpose of the law? What does it do to you or for you? Are you happy when you think about it? Do you spend a lot of time meditating on it as did the psalmist of old? And what do we mean when we mouth the phrase, We "are not under the law, but under grace," quoting the apostle Paul (Romans 6:14)?

There is good news and bad news for those seeking answers to their questions about the law. In Romans 9 and 10, the apostle Paul speaks about the law as a method for salvation. "Brethren, my heart's desire and prayer to God for Israel is, that they might be saved" (Romans 10:1). Now, who is this talking about? Israel? Who *is* Israel today? Those who believe. "If ye be Christ's, then are ye Abraham's seed" (Galatians 3:29).

> My heart's desire . . . is that they [all Israel] might be saved. For I bear them record that they have a zeal of God, but not according to knowledge. For they being ignorant of God's righteousness, and going about to establish their own righteousness, have not submitted themselves unto the righteousness of God. For Christ is the end of the law for righteousness to every one that believeth (Romans 10:1-4).

There's another way of reading this last phrase—"Christ is the goal of the law." Christ really is the fulfillment of the law. He is also the end of the law for righteousness by works. But He is not the end of the law itself.

24

As we consider God's law and particularly His Ten Commandments, we need to notice that they have some very definite functions and purposes. One of those great functions and purposes is to protect us.

One day I was driving across the desert between California and Texas, and suddenly my Honda Accord gave up the ghost. Yes, it had a lot of miles on it, but it hadn't shown any signs of old age or illness. However, no one had told me (and I didn't read the manual) that the engine coolant is supposed to be changed every year or so. And I had never changed it. So, a chemical reaction of some kind had developed on the aluminum piston heads and given them the chickenpox. The head gasket blew, and the engine overheated and locked up. If I only had read the manual or if someone had told me! But there I sat in the desert, paying a pretty big price for being ignorant of the rules.

God's Ten-Commandment law is the manual, our manual for life. Fiorello La Guardia of New York City, the famous mayor of yesteryear, said that while lawyers and legislators have made ten thousand laws, they have never made a single improvement on the Ten Commandments. Don't you agree?

I like this short, joyful version of the Ten Commandments put to rhyme:

Above all else, love God alone,
Bow down to neither wood nor stone.
God's name, refuse to take in vain,
The Sabbath rest with care maintain.
Respect your parents all your days,
Hold sacred human life always.
Be loyal to your chosen mate,
Steal nothing either small or great.
Report with truth your neighbor's deed,
And rid your mind of selfish greed.

Not bad! How could anyone get a more concise, beautiful description of the manual for life?

God's law has several other legitimate functions in addition to protecting us.

We are under the law as a standard for salvation. Not as a method to achieve salvation, but a standard. It is a standard by which we are judged, according to James 2:8-13.

We are under the condemnation of the law. Even though we don't like it and it seems painful, it is a legitimate function of the law (see Romans 4:15). Some people get uncomfortable with this condemnation idea and try to come up with rationalizations to do away with it.

The law is as eternal as God Himself. If you don't respect law, then anarchy follows. I heard it this way on the old sawdust trail: "No government is any stronger than its laws, and no law is any stronger than the penalty for breaking it, and no penalty is any stronger than the enforcement of the penalty for breaking it." But for those who haven't gotten past Mount Sinai, the law must be bondage and nothing but condemnation.

We are under the curse of the law, which is another painful realization. But it is a legitimate function of law. Galatians 3:13 says, "Cursed is everyone who is hung on a tree" (NIV). Isn't it good news to know that Jesus took that curse in our place?

According to Galatians 3:24, 25, the law is also a schoolmaster to lead us to Christ. The apostle Paul spoke of the law in this way: "By the law is the knowledge of sin" (Romans 3:20). It leads us to the foot of the cross. And in James 1:23, 25, the law is compared to a mirror that shows us our need for washing or cleansing.

So there are a number of legitimate uses of God's law in Scripture. It can either bring pain or it can bring comfort and hope by taking us to the cross for cleansing.

There is one illegitimate use of the law that the apostle Paul speaks vehemently against: Using the law as a method for salvation—or legalism, as we call it today. Now, I suppose we could debate the meaning of the word *legalism*.

A friend of mine, Mary Walsh, who worked in evangelism with my parents for years, is a dedicated Bible instructor. I understand she is still going strong, waking people in the morning and at night to study the Bible. She gets unhappy with people who talk against legalism. She says, "I am a legalist."

"What do you mean?" I ask.

"Well, I believe in the law of God. And anyone who believes in the law of God is a legalist."

"Well," I say, "OK, OK. If that's your definition of legalism, then I'm a legalist because I too believe in the law of God."

But, in its common usage today, I'm going to hazard a different definition. I hope it lines up with what you're used to thinking. Legalism is an attempt to get to heaven by keeping God's law. Basically, it's an attempt to save myself by my own works. So, legalism would be salvation by works, salvation by law, or salvation by good behavior, trying to live a little better this year than I did last year, trying to get my act together before the final events begin.

In another, more important sense, there is a deeper definition of legalism that we ought to consider seriously. It is not having a faith relationship with Christ. There are really only three kinds of people in the world. First, there are those who are not interested in God or faith or salvation. Perhaps they're not even in the ballpark of this discussion. We wouldn't call them legalists or anything else. They're just not interested.

In the second group are those who are interested in salvation and have a personal daily relationship with Jesus.

Those in the third group hope for salvation. In theory, they are against legalism. They are not interested in trying to work themselves to heaven. But they have no relationship with Christ. They pay no attention to the faith experience, so they are still legalists. Because anyone, regardless of his words or theology, who has no time for the daily faith experience with Christ is a legalist. There are no other options.

Either you are in Christ, in fellowship with Him, or you are a legalist. You might *say*, "I am not a legalist; I do not believe in working my way to heaven." But if you don't have a vital connection with Christ, there are no other options. It's either one or the other (unless you are out of the ballpark, not concerned with salvation at all).

I can say that I don't believe in legalism, that I believe in righteousness through faith in Christ. And I may, in theory. But, if I do not become involved in it in *practice*, then I don't believe in it at all. Isn't that true? I don't have to tell my wife I don't love her. All I have to do is never come home. She'll get the message. I don't have to tell God I don't love Him, or I don't believe in faith. All I have to do is have no time for Him or the things of faith, and He'll get the message. And I will be entrenched in the thing we call legalism.

There are, of course, two kinds of legalists. There is the rigid, conservative, hard-core, fundamental legalist who wears the black suit and the black tie and the black socks and the black shoes. He judges everybody else who doesn't live up to his standard. He seems very unhappy and shows no mercy, no love.

Then there is the liberal legalist. He is the loose legalist who still has no relationship with Christ or time for the things of faith. He is trying to work his way to heaven by the things he doesn't do that the legalist does do. So the liberal legalist finds his security in the standards and rules of the church that he abandons. He's sure that he's not a legalist because he doesn't do these things that the rigid ones do. "I have been emancipated from that. I can go where I want, eat what I please, drink what I like, do whatever feels good. I am not a legalist anymore." But he is a liberal legalist.

So the pure definition of a legalist is anyone who claims to be a Christian and hopes to be saved in heaven, but is living life, rigidly or liberally, apart from Christ.

The apostle Paul talked vehemently against this again and again. But he gave us opportunity to consider something far better. He invited us to accept Christ as the end of the law for righteousness and to focus instead on Jesus as our only hope for salvation.

At a camp meeting we were visiting, our little daughter was taken into the kindergarten division. As part of the lesson that day the teacher said, "What is it that is the most important in all the Bible?" And the boys and girls in the kindergarten division said, "Jesus, Jesus." The teacher said, "No, no, I don't mean that. What is it that is the most important in all the Bible?" Silence. Finally, she gave them the answer, "It's the Ten Commandments. That is the most important in all the Bible." True or False?

My wife complained to the division leader after the service, because that's the kind of teaching that keeps our boys and girls on the behavior-centered path that so many are used to: "If you're good, you go to heaven; if you're bad, Jesus won't love you."

When are we going to realize that the most important focus in all the Bible is Jesus? Well, the division leader, trying to apologize for the teacher, said, "She was tired today; she was tired." And when I heard that, it rang a bell. Because there was a time in my life when I thought that the Ten Commandments were the most important. And I got tired too. If you think that the primary focus of the Bible is the Ten Commandments, you're going to get very tired.

Right here people get nervous and say, "This man is against the Ten Commandments." No, I am not against the Ten Commandments any more than E. J. Waggoner was against the Ten Commandments. Have you heard of him? E. J. Waggoner, in the 1890s, was a champion of salvation through faith alone in Jesus Christ. At that time, it was said that we had preached the law until we were as dry as the hills of Gilboa and that we needed to preach Christ in the law. We were not to bypass the law, because the path to the Promised Land goes past Mount Sinai. But Waggoner was charged, as all righteousness-by-faith preachers are, with being antinomian, or against God's law. And this was his response: "Instead of faith leading to antinomianism (or being against God's law), it is the only thing that is contrary to antinomianism. It matters not how much a person boasts in the law of God. If he rejects or ignores implicit faith in Christ, he is in no better state than the one who directly attacks the law."

This is ironic. The person who champions the law of God and raises the Ten Commandments to the highest level is the one who is actually against the Ten Commandments. Why? Because there is no power in the Ten Commandments to save a person. When La Guardia said, "Mankind has made ten thousand laws, but he's never made a single improvement on the Ten Commandments," he was wrong in one way. Because there was one man who made improvement on the Ten Commandments. His name was Jesus. He came and showed the Ten Commandments made up into a life.

In Jesus, there was a heart that cared. There is no heart in the Ten Commandments when they condemn us. There is a heart in the Ten Commandments in terms of protection. But there was no hope for poor sinners facing Mount Sinai until One came and showed the Ten Commandments made up into a life. He had a heart that cared for sinners and harlots and thieves and nit-picking Pharisees and legalists and scribes. So, we see in Jesus a tremendous improvement on the Ten Commandments.

It matters not how much a person boasts in the law of God; if he rejects or ignores implicit faith in Christ, he is in no better state than the one who directly assails the law. The man of faith is the only one who truly honors the law of God. Without faith it is impossible to please God (Hebrews 11:6); with it, all things are possible (Mark 9:23).

Yes, faith does the impossible, and it is just that which God requires us to do. When Joshua said to Israel, "Ye cannot serve the Lord," he told the truth; yet it was a fact that God required them to serve Him. It is not within any man's power to do righteousness [and keep the commandments], even though he wants to (Galatians 5:17); therefore it is a mistake to say that all God wants is for us to do the best we can. He who does no better than that will not do the works of God. No, he must *do better than he can do*. He must do that which only the power of God working through him can do. It is impossible for a man to walk on water, but Peter did it when he exercised faith in Jesus.

Since all power in heaven and in earth is in the hands of Christ, and this power is at our disposal, even Christ Himself coming to dwell in the heart by faith, there is no room for finding fault with God for requiring us to do the impossible; for "the things which are impossible with men are possible with God" (E. J. Waggoner, *Christ and His Righteousness*, pp. 95, 96).

So let's nail it down. The only person who is really interested in, and is in favor of, the Ten Commandments is the one who puts Jesus as the most important in all the Bible. And that's the only way one exalts the law of God. There is no other way.

For a long time Seventh-day Adventists have been called legalists, probably because of the Sabbath. People say, "You think you're going to get to heaven by keeping the Sabbath." And so they call us legalists. Let me ask you, do you know of anyone who has ever been called a legalist because he didn't believe in stealing? Do you know of anyone who has ever been called a legalist because he didn't believe in killing or lying or cheating? I haven't met one yet. It's interesting, isn't it? So, whether I am being called a legalist or calling someone else a legalist, it's important to get the definition straight.

Let's remember something else that is extremely significant in Scripture. All ten of the commandments hang together. It has always been interesting to me, as a Seventh-day Adventist, that right in the middle of His Ten Commandment law, God put something in honor of the Creator, a day of worship. So the fancy footwork that people sometimes are inclined to do, to try to dissect the Ten Commandments and get one of them out of there, just won't work. It's all one unit.

"Oh," someone says, "you're a legalist because you're trying to get to heaven like the Jews did. The Sabbath is something for the Jews." No, it goes all the way back to Creation twenty-five hundred years before the first Jew, Father Abraham.

If you look carefully at Hebrews 4, you will discover that the Sabbath, right in the middle of God's Ten Commandment law, is actually one of the greatest symbols of salvation through faith in Christ. Sabbath and rest are synonymous. Christ offers us rest from trying to save ourselves. Paul says, "Christ is the end of the law for righteousness" (Romans 10:4). That means at least two things. He's the end of my trying to

31

do anything to get rid of my guilt, to get my sins forgiven. I cannot earn or merit that. And He's the end of my trying to work hard to overcome my sins, because He has offered me rest on that level as well.

Victory and obedience and overcoming are gifts from Him. Christ is the end of the law for righteousness *for* me and the end of the law for righteousness *in* me. Christ is the end of it all. And He is a beautiful example of the one who proved it by His own life.

The apostle Paul gives us a clue as to how we can get away from being married to the law and be married to Christ instead. In the first few verses of Roman 7, he talks about being married to the law, with the law actually being the husband. But, he says, there is something better. Let's see if you can roll with this parable.

Everyone respected *Law*rence. (Laurence? No, *Law*rence. OK?) In all of his wide circle of acquaintances you could hardly have found one who wouldn't admit that Lawrence really had it all together. Christina was sure that their marriage would be one that was made in heaven. She recognized Lawrences's many fine qualities, and she had learned to, well, not exactly love him, but she certainly respected him highly. She was sure that love would come as they spent more time together. The day of the wedding arrived, the soft music began to play, and Christina walked up to the altar to make her public commitment to Lawrence. She promised to remain faithful to him until death would them part, and then Christina and Lawrence were pronounced husband and wife. (Married to the *Law*rence! OK?)

But even before the honeymoon was over, the problems began. By the time they moved into their new house, it was most apparent that they didn't like the same things at all. Christina became increasingly unhappy with Lawrence. He wasn't the least bit tolerant. His ideas were set in concrete. She soon gave up even trying to argue with him. It wasn't that he forced her to do things his way. But, he was always there looking at her reproachfully, whenever she would try to unbend and be herself. She grew increasingly weary of his constant condemnation. He not only made judgments about her outward behavior, he judged her inward motives as well.

Christina tried everything to please him. Day after day, she would wake up grimly determined that this would be the day that Lawrence would be pleased with her. But while she was taking extra pains to make one thing perfect, she would discover that something else had been neglected. And there were times when all of her best efforts ended in total disaster. It seemed that the harder she tried, the more mistakes she made.

On occasion, Christina became so discouraged that she adopted a devil-may-care attitude and went rashly through the day, doing exactly as she pleased. She took an almost fiendish delight in leaving clothes on the floor and dishes in the sink, while she spent time watching movies on TV and eating chocolates and potato chips by the handful. But nothing changed. Apart from weight, the only thing Christina ever gained, no matter what approach she tried, was a growing awareness of how far she fell short of Lawrence's ideals. Always she could feel his eyes upon her, judging, accusing, and condemning.

One night, as she lay quietly beside him in bed, she felt that she could not possibly stand her life, the way it was, for even one more day. Lawrence, who had seemed so worthy of her respect and honor at her marriage, now seemed ugly and hateful. She could never please him. It was hopeless to try. There was no way she could measure up even for one day, much less for the lifetime she had promised. If only she could be married to someone else, someone who would approve of her and love her the way she was. But the words "till death do us part" echoed in her mind.

Suddenly she had a bright idea. Lawrence was sleeping quietly beside her. If she could somehow manage to . . . but how? She soon realized it was impossible for her to kill him. She wasn't strong enough. But wait. If she couldn't kill him, maybe she could kill herself. What was life worth, anyway, if it had to be lived like this?! But to her dismay, she didn't have the strength or courage to kill herself either. Yet she couldn't

33

go on any longer. If only she could die and be resurrected to start life over! If only she could begin again!

In utter despair, realizing there was nothing at all she could do to help herself, she cried out, "God, if anything gets done to save me from this awful mess, You're going to have to do it, and You're going to have to do it all." For the first time in years, she felt peace and she fell asleep.

Christina awakened early the next morning. Lawrence was still there, apparently. Yet everything seemed somehow different. Perhaps the one beside her was Lawrence's twin brother. The tenderness in his eyes and beautiful lines on his face spoke of a struggle he'd been through. And there were scars in his hands that Christina had somehow not noticed before. Instead of rushing out into the kitchen, she began the day by taking time to communicate with Lawrence. Later that very day, she found herself singing as she did her housework and polished the silverware.

As the days went by, Christina spent more time getting to know this person. She could hardly wait for the next opportunity to spend special time alone with him, for he loved her just as she was and accepted her even while she was making mistakes. And somehow the more love and acceptance she felt, the less she worried about her actions and the fewer mistakes she made. Lawrence's demands just didn't seem as unreasonable as they had before.

Then one day, it struck her. Her whole relationship had changed. Not only did she find pleasure in pleasing him, but her own interests and inclinations were changing. She now was beginning to love the things he loved. Once she had thought that only if Lawrence died could she find peace. But, it was Christina who had died and been resurrected to walk in newness of life.

Chapter
Three

Your Money Where Your Mouth Is

Martin Luther should have paid more attention to the apostle James. James basically said, "Don't just talk faith; prove it by your actions." "Put your money where your mouth is." "Actions speak louder than words." I want to write about good works in the Christian life, but it can be a very ticklish subject. Should it even come up? Whatever happened to individual standards and church standards? Are we supposed to have any?

In the popular version of salvation through faith, with its emphasis on God's love, forgiveness, and acceptance, there is a tendency to toss these terms around like slogans. But something significant was penned years ago to our church: "The righteousness of Christ is not a cloak to cover unconfessed and unforsaken sin; it is a principle of life that transforms the character and controls the conduct" (*The Desire of Ages*, pp. 555, 556).

Righteousness by faith, if it is real, will not make me less of a Christian; it will make me more of one. It won't make me less interested in genuine obedience and good works; it will make me more interested. It won't make me less of an Adventist. If I really understand what it's all about, it will make me more of a real Adventist. So, in our atmosphere today of simply sloganizing salvation by faith and God's love and forgiveness and acceptance, we must understand the place and value of good works. Before we get further into the question of standards and ethics, we need to address the topic of *works* in the Christian life.

In the history of the Christian church, councils discussing faith and works have met again and again over the centuries. Some have split churches right down the middle. It would be easier to neglect this subject, to ignore it, or to forget it. But knowing what the Scriptures teach on this subject is vital to understanding what God expects in our relationship to Him.

First of all, is there any doubt that the subject of good works shows up in Scripture alongside faith? In the famous text that we use again and again in our support of salvation only through faith, Ephesians 2:8, 9, we read, "By grace are ye saved through faith; and that not of yourselves: it is the gift of God: not of works, lest any man should boast." But sometimes we don't read how the same passage goes on to say that we were created for good works.

Galatians 2:16 says, "A man is not justified by the works of the law, but by the faith of Jesus Christ." But the apostle Paul adds, "Do we then make void the law through faith? God forbid" (Romans 3:31). The Bible tells us in Titus 2:14, Jesus "gave himself for us, that he might redeem us from all iniquity, and purify unto himself a peculiar people, zealous of good works." 2 Timothy 3:16, 17: "All scripture is given by inspiration of God, and is profitable for doctrine, for reproof, for correction, for instruction in righteousness: that the man of God may be perfect, thoroughly furnished *unto all good works*" (emphasis supplied). And "We are his workmanship, created in Christ Jesus unto good works" (Ephesians 2:10). So, if you look for it, you'll find works showing up again and again in Scripture.

I checked with my computer (it reads the whole Bible in three seconds), and there were 120 texts that deal directly with works. I discovered that there are bad works and good works described in Scripture. There are also bad people and good people mentioned in Scripture. So perhaps we could divide people and works into these four categories:

Is it possible for bad works to be done by bad people? Of course.

Is it possible for bad works to be done by good people? Yes.

Is it possible for good works to be done by bad people?

Is it possible for good works to be done by good people?

Well, now, with the topic neatly divided, which group do you want to be in? What about bad works done by bad people? Who comes to mind when you read this question? Consider the people who crucified Jesus. Who were they, bad people or good people?

"There is none good, no not one" (see Romans 3:10). All right, they were bad people. But they sure looked like good people, didn't they? So, this leads, of course, into the question, What is it that makes you a good person or a bad person? Is it what you *do* that makes you good or bad?

Picture Judas betraying Jesus. He was a bad person, doing a bad deed, at least at that point in his life. But before that, for a long period of time, he looked like a good person. In fact, it seems that he cast out devils, healed the sick, cleansed the lepers, and raised the dead, just like the other disciples. So, he must have been operating from God's goodness during that time. But he walked away from it.

What about bad works done by good people? Do we have any of that in Scripture? I think of Peter. Was Peter a good person? In context, yes, Peter was a good person. Take a look at him in the immediate context of the day just before Jesus died. They had finished the famous Last Supper in the upper room, and Jesus had said to them, "Now ye are clean" (see John 13:10). They were clean, through the word that He had spoken to them. He had given them the good news of forgiveness and cleansing from sin. But just a little bit later, Peter was swinging his sword, trying to cut off people's ears (or at least one). Was that a bad work, done by a clean person? Check with the high priest's servant about how bad it was. I

37

think that he would be happy to admit that this was a bad deed. It must have hurt, at least. But it was done by a good person. What was bad about what he did, the deed itself, or his reason for doing it—taking things into his own hands, depending upon himself instead of trusting God?

Jesus said, "Put up your sword. . . . If my kingdom was of this world then would my servants fight" (John 18:11, 36). But His kingdom is not of this world. So, the bad thing about Peter was not necessarily the deed, although the high priest's servant might not agree. It was that he was trying to "do it himself." That is the real issue in sin.

But Peter was still a good person. The disciples were good according to Jesus' "Now ye are clean" statement. They were good because of His righteousness. But they did some bad things during the time that they walked with Jesus. So, what is it that makes a person bad?

There was a man in Philadelphia who was arrested because he stole bread to feed his family. In court, the evidence showed that he was a good man, trying to help his family, but he had done a bad deed. The judge recognized this and fined him for his bad deed. However, he immediately suspended the sentence and passed the hat in the courtroom, making everyone donate money as a penalty for living in a town where a man would have to steal bread to feed his family. Then he gave the collected money to the man.

The judge must have been operating a little like God does. Or, was he? Is it always, always, wrong to steal? Regardless of the reason? This is part of the sticky territory we have to consider here. You cannot talk about right and wrong, about good deeds and bad deeds, unless you get into this question of morality, including the new morality.

Are you familiar with new morality? It's called situation ethics, taking the position that it is all right to do bad things as long as you do them for good reasons.

Or do you agree with the kind of preaching I grew up listening to, that used to say, loud, long, and clear, "It is always, always, wrong to steal; it is always, always, wrong to lie or cheat or kill"? Or is that too simple? We need to explore some

38

of these areas when we get into this subject of right and wrong and moral judgments.

Is it possible for good works to be done by bad people? Immediately, we think of Matthew 7:21, 22, where Jesus said:

> Not every one that saith unto me, Lord, Lord, shall enter into the kingdom of heaven; but he that doeth the will of my Father which is in heaven. Many will say to me in that day, Lord, Lord, have we not prophesied in thy name? and in thy name have cast out devils? and in thy name done many wonderful works?

And in verse 23, "And then will I profess unto them, I never knew you: depart from me, ye that work iniquity." You mean prophesying in His name is iniquity? Casting out devils is iniquity? Doing many wonderful works is iniquity? What was it that made these people's deeds bad?

These verses focus in on something extremely crucial. Because we are born bad, the only way we can ever experience any kind of goodness is through Jesus. So, what makes people bad is living apart from Christ, regardless of what they do. And what makes people good is living in relationship with Christ, regar . . . regar . . . re . . . I have a hard time going that far, because someone will misunderstand . . . regardless of what they do? Do you *ever* judge people, in terms of whether they are bad or good, by their actions *only*? Or do you, again, look at them through relationship glasses?

I took the position one time that good works done apart from Christ are bad works. I got shot out of the water. People said, "You can't say that! Good works done apart from Christ are not bad works, because the works themselves are good." So, I've changed my position. Good works done apart from Christ are bad, period. Not that they are bad works, but they are bad.

Why are they bad? Here are two reasons, listed in Matthew 7. In the first place, these people claimed: "Have we not prophesied in thy name, cast out devils in thy name, and done many wonderful works in thy name?" But they never *knew* Jesus. So, essentially they were liars. To claim to do good works in

39

Christ's name, if I don't know Him, makes me a liar. It's all a deception. The only person who is really operating in Jesus' name is the one who is in vital relationship with Him. Apart from that, claiming to be a Christian, claiming to be operating in His name, is pretense and deception. So, that's the first thing that made them guilty of iniquity.

The second problem was that these people had fallen into the trap of thinking that they were going to heaven *because* they prophesied and cast out devils and did many wonderful works. The pit of salvation by works, again. It's been a problem in the church for a long, long time. To think that I can in any way save myself, even 10 percent, is a lie and is iniquity. Paul says we're not saved by works; if we were, then we'd have some reason to boast. Have you ever backed up and taken a look at some of the boasting that we do?

Even in the setting of the Christian church, we can give evidence that we are living apart from God. One of the first evidences that shows up is the constant rising of self to the top. Paul says, if I am going to boast, I had better boast in front of people who believe in salvation by works. (I am paraphrasing him. See Romans 2:17-23.) If I want to get some credit, and if I want to give some credit, then I had better make sure that I am talking to people who believe in the merit system. Otherwise they are not going to thank me for it. As far as God is concerned, there is no room for us to boast. And the closer I get to Jesus, the lower I get at the foot of the cross. Kneeling in faith and in humility at the foot of the cross is the highest place that I can ever reach.

So, Paul makes it clear, there is no room for boasting. "Oh, but I've cast out devils." "Are you sure?" You know, if I were the devil and I read in the Bible what Jesus said, that Satan cannot cast out Satan, I would really specialize in that one. I'd say, that really gives me cover. I can move in on that! I don't believe the devil casts out the devils, but I believe the devil knows how to make it appear that he casts out the devils.

I suppose you've heard of the deliverance ministry. I am praying that God will continue to deliver us from the deliverance ministry because the deliverance ministry, with the way it emerged in the evangelical churches and tried to jump into our denomination, was not casting out devils at all. It simply appeared that way for a while. And the devil is very happy to apparently cast out devils—and substitute something worse in the process. So, casting out devils, even if it is real, is no room for me to boast. Because I should know, by now, that devils are bigger than I am and whoever really casts them out is bigger than I—none other than the Lord Jesus Himself.

What about prophesying? Is that a good thing? Recently, I heard that the Adventist church in France disfellowshiped a so-called prophet who was sending out messages. After taking a long look at this situation and checking out the fruits and the messages, the church has taken a dim view concerning someone over there who pretended to be a prophet.

There was a prophetess who moved from Florida to Oregon several years ago. I listened to some of the tapes of her prophecy, supposedly in Jesus' name. But after a while, you can begin to pick telltale evidence that these people are boasting in their manifestations. And when people begin to tell of their works and to advertise their successes, they immediately come into question. Don't they? Doing good works. Is that bad? No, not if the works are really good. But if I want credit for them, that makes them bad.

Let's desire to be people with the type of mentality that wants to do good works because we have discovered the Good Person. And if you check it out, I think you'll discover that for the person who is really good, the one who knows Jesus as his or her personal friend, the good works spring forth spontaneously. These works are not calculated, they are not deliberate. These are not the kind of people who say, when someone comes for help, "Wait till we have a crowd at the tent or the auditorium," or, "Wait till the television cameras are here." They are the kind of people who operate as Jesus operated. When He did a good deed, even raising the dead, He disappeared shortly after. He wasn't looking for praise and honor. He wanted all the glory and all the credit to go to His Father.

41

Wouldn't you like to have God lead you to be a good person, because of Jesus' goodness? And for your good works to spring forth naturally and spontaneously as a result?

Years ago, as a college student, I was at a Bible conference at the Sligo Church in Takoma Park, Maryland, for which H. M. S. Richards gave the devotional message. I'll never forget his text. He was reading from Acts about Barnabas, of whom it was said, "He was a good man, and full of the Holy Ghost and of faith: and much people was added unto the Lord" (Acts 11:24).

And the radio preacher simply dwelt a little while on that verse. "You know," he said, "when I am gone, I hope that people won't remember me as the radio preacher or anything else great." He said, "I would like to be remembered as a good man. In my family, I hope when they think of me, they think of me as a good man." Maybe that is not a bad ambition—to be a good man, a good woman, a good person full of the Holy Ghost. And if that happens, "much people" are going to be added to the Lord.

The Bible speaks about the works of the law and the works of faith. These two designations are very clear. Sometimes they show up as evil works versus good works, or dead works versus alive works. But the basic labels are works of the law and works of faith. I suppose, in one sense, we can say that the works of the law are those we are trying to do in order to be saved. And the apostle Paul says, these are dead works. I would like to define them in this fashion: works of the law are any works done apart from a faith relationship with Christ. And they are dead. They are worthless as far as God is concerned.

Works of faith are the good works done in the setting of a relationship with Christ. Now, people who are in that relationship sometimes have good works and sometimes bad works. And the people who are outside of that relationship sometimes have good works and sometimes have bad works. But the main issue is being in Christ or outside of Christ.

The Bible also addresses the purpose of good works in the life of the Christian. And it comes down really heavy on this point: good works are never for the purpose of saving us in heaven. A. T. Jones, in the 1890s, got up and said, "Works amount to nothing." And he was reproved for his strong statement. To say that works have nothing to do with salvation is wrong. I would like to add one word in an attempt to correct that sentence. Our good works have nothing to do with *causing* our salvation. But they do have something to do with salvation. And here is the reason. Good works are always the result of genuine faith in Christ. And the purpose of good works is to glorify God. "Let your light so shine before men, that they may see your good works, and glorify your Father which is in heaven" (Matthew 5:16). It just so happens that saved people want to glorify God. If they don't want to glorify God, that is pretty good evidence they haven't been saved. The two go together.

And this, of course, is James's point. James makes it clear that faith and works go together like love and marriage, and "Love and marriage go together like a horse and carriage" (That's a song from the forties, isn't it? Or the thirties?). I guess the illustration doesn't hold too tight anymore in terms of love and marriage. And I haven't seen too many horses and carriages around lately, either. I've tried to figure out some other illustrations about two things that always go together. Thunder and lightning, perhaps (but the closer they are together the worse it is, you know).

Thunder and lightning don't always go together, though. With heat lightning, you don't hear the thunder. So, someone came up with a better illustration—sunshine and shadow. Except for the people who live in Seattle (it's almost always cold and rainy in Seattle). When asked what they do in the summer, people from Seattle say, "Well, if it comes on a Sunday, we go fishing." So maybe we should change the illustration to simply light and shadow. They always go together.

Faith and works go together, according to James. You cannot separate them. Genuine faith is going to produce genuine works. Maybe that's why the Bible can talk about being judged by and rewarded by our works. God didn't intend, through His prophets and His godly writers, to give the impression that we are in any way saved by our works. But if faith and works always exist together, never apart and never alone, then if you say we are saved by works, you are really saying we're saved by faith. In addition, of course, God is capable of judging us and rewarding us according to our works, because He knows the motives behind our works.

One graveside service I held was next to the fresh grave of a member of the Hell's Angels motorcycle gang. The tombstone on his grave boasted these words: "Forever A Rebel." What an epitaph! I was immediately angry. I wanted to get rid of that grave and the tombstone and the whole business. Who would want to shout out to the world "forever a rebel"? Then I began to think, only God knows what made him tick. When our young people have rebelled from the church because they have heard too much of righteousness by the works of the law, only God knows their hearts and can judge them. Aren't you glad we're in better hands than ours, when it come to judging people's actions?

James made it clear that if you really have faith, you're going to prove it by putting your money where your mouth is. James is not talking about what *causes* our salvation, as Paul is. That's a point we often miss. James is talking about how to tell if a person has genuine faith. And how can you tell? If a person has genuine faith, he is interested in good works—God's good works, not his.

It is encouraging that God's works can become my works. Listen to these interesting insights:

> Lord, thou wilt ordain peace for us: for thou also hast wrought all our works in us (Isaiah 26:12).

> It is God which worketh in you both to will and to do of his good pleasure (Philippians 2:13).

> Now the God of peace, that brought again from the dead our Lord Jesus, that great shepherd of the sheep, through the blood of the everlasting covenant, make you perfect in every good work to do his will, working in you that which is wellpleasing in his sight (Hebrews 13:20, 21).

I am interested in good works—His! Aren't you? Let's pray and study, as the church struggles with this issue, that we don't end up with slogans about salvation that let us escape good works. Rather, let us look for real salvation through faith, love, forgiveness, and acceptance, including God's good works that go with it.

Four

Black, White, or Gray
Part One

I don't like neckties, but they do provide a convenient place to hang the microphone when I speak in church. Sometimes I get up in the morning before my wife, then later in the day, when I get back home, she looks at the clashing color of the tie I have chosen, and she says, "You didn't really wear that, did you?" And I have to confess that I did. But I wear a necktie in church because I don't want to offend anyone. There are some people who would be offended and think it not proper for me to preach without my necktie. Right?

When it comes to real obedience, how do we decide between right and wrong? How do we establish church standards and personal ethics? In reading the title "Black, White, or Gray," I hope you don't assume any racial overtones. I chose it on purpose, because most of us are familiar with trying to decide right or wrong. Most of us are familiar with the black area, doing the wrong thing for the wrong reason (like killing six million Jews for fun, or because I hate them). Or, the white area, doing the right thing for the right reason (like going to church because I love God).

But the gray areas confuse us. Even trying to decide which areas are gray is difficult. Maybe we can begin by saying that gray areas would be doing the right thing for the wrong reason or doing the wrong thing for the right reason. But in a gray area, what method do you use to decide what is right or wrong?

I have noted, from personal study, personal experience, and case histories, that the devil loves gray areas. He never takes people from white to black in one big jump. He moves them through the gray. Isn't that true? No one turns from an innocent babe to a murderous criminal overnight. The downward path that the devil loves to use is always gradual. And those downward steps are often through gray areas. We might not be able to see anything at all wrong with step one except that it leads to step two, and often we don't even notice that until we look back.

Let's begin with the question of personal ethics and standards. Then perhaps we will better understand how to address church ethics and church standards.

People are accustomed to deciding right and wrong in a number of ways. Probably one of the oldest is, "Oh, let's just stay in the middle of the road." One of the biggest problems in the Christian church today is the large number of middle-of-the-road moderates who cannot lay down their cross because they never took it up. In the church known in Revelation as Laodicea (lukewarm), the middle of the road could be the wrong place to be. Isn't that true? In the lukewarm church (and most of us, according to prophecy, are liable to be in that church just before Jesus comes), the appropriate place on the road might not be in the middle.

Some people claim, "One way to decide right or wrong is to always do what Jesus would do." And there have been whole books written on this subject, like *The Imitation of Christ* by Thomas à Kempis. Or Charles Sheldon's book, *In His Steps*, in which a whole church decided they were going to do what Jesus would do. But, our understanding of what Jesus would do is heavily influenced by our own backgrounds, our frame of reference, and our culture. There are many different ideas on what Jesus would do. I know conservative Christians who think it's wrong to bowl and to shoot pool. And I know other Christians, who apparently are just as interested in Christ, who think it is perfectly all right. It depends on how you were brought up. So, simply asking the question "What would Jesus do?" might not be enough.

Then you have people who write letters to the *Adventist Review* asking whether it's all right to bake potatoes in the oven on Sabbath. I, as a pastor, have been called on the phone by church members wanting to find out the answers to these kinds of questions. I always have a hard time with such questions, and I say, "To your knees, my friend, to your knees, and to your own closet!" Getting an answer from church headquarters is typical of one of the world's giant churches, not known for having trained its people to think. And even in that giant church there have been some changes in recent years where people are being encouraged to think (thank the Lord for that).

Another approach to deciding between right and wrong says, "What is everyone else doing? What is the crowd doing?" I hope we understand how naive that approach is. I was driving along the nicely divided Ohio turnpike one time, when the center line between the two lanes on my side was being painted. There were signs along the road that said, "Don't pass!"

Eventually, I got tired of driving behind someone who wasn't going anywhere fast. So, when the car immediately in front of me moved out and passed (getting white paint on his tires), I moved out and passed too. And so did the police officer behind me. He pulled us both over. After he'd given the man ahead of me a ticket, he asked me, "Why did you pass the car?" I said, "Because that man ahead of me did." He replied, "If he jumped off the Brooklyn Bridge, would you jump too?" And I realized, on the Ohio Turnpike, how foolish it is to do something simply because other people are doing it.

So, what is your method of trying to decide between right

49

and wrong, particularly when it comes to the gray areas? How do you decide personal standards, especially in areas like music, entertainment, books, TV, dress, and appearance?

The typical standards of the Christian church came over from the last century, and many people today delight in shooting at them. In fact, so much of what we hear about them is negative, that I thought, maybe, it would be good to have a look at them from the positive side. I want to talk in favor of personal ethics and Christian standards and maybe even church standards.

If we go to the Bible, we find a text that speaks to the issue, but it is not complete enough.

Love not the world, neither the things that are in the world. If any man love the world, the love of the Father is not in him. For all that is in the world, the lust of the flesh, and the lust of the eyes, and the pride of life, is not of the Father, but is of the world. And the world passeth away, and the lust thereof: but he that doeth the will of God abideth for ever (1 John 2:15-17).

"Love not the world, neither the things that are in the world." It is a good principle. But if I lived in Pennsylvania today, or even certain parts of Iowa and Missouri, I would find that it is wrong to have a car, and I would still be driving down the road with my horse and buggy. Why? Because some of those communities consider it worldly to have a car. I had a friend who felt it was extravagant to wear a watch. "That is of the world," he said. So, again, your view of right and wrong comes down to the influence of your background, your subculture, your own thinking. How are you going to define "the world"?

We often hear people say, "God has given us minds to think. Why don't we use the brains that He has given us?" When we consider this approach, we go back to the Garden of Eden, where the serpent said to the woman at the tree, "Go ahead and eat. You can become as God, knowing good and evil" (see Genesis 3:4, 5). Maybe an application of that old story comes into the picture here. Do you really think that you are God and that you can decide between good and evil all on your own thinking, with your own logic and reason? Or isn't it a painful reality that most of our logic and reason can only deal with outward actions? Therein lies the problem. The Bible says that people look on the outward appearance but God looks where? At the heart (see 1 Samuel 16:7).

Proverbs tells us that it is extremely important to consider the issues of the heart. And when the Bible speaks of the heart, it is speaking of the mind, the inward motives and purposes. "Keep thy heart with all diligence; for out of it are the issues of life" (Proverbs 4:23). And Jesus made it clear to the Pharisees, who were trying to be clean and spotless on the outside, that this is comparatively insignificant when we consider the inside.

Maybe one of the best ways to understand the gray areas, and why we do what we do, would be to examine the inside. But who is up to this? The Bible says, "The heart is deceitful above all things, and desperately wicked: who can know it?" (Jeremiah 17:9). So, are we even capable of trying to understand why we do what we do? Obviously, God doesn't just look at what we do; He looks at why we do what we do. And that's good news. So wouldn't it be worthwhile to ask Him to help us understand why we do what we do? This could be the deciding factor in determining whether an issue is black or white, as we approach the gray.

Another guideline that helps me in terms of my relationship to the Christian community is found in 1 Thessalonians 5:22, where Paul says to the Christian church, "Abstain from all the appearance of evil." Apparently there are some things that are not evil but appear evil. And he says, avoid them. Again, I am talking about principles, not details, because I am very much aware that the details can polarize the Christian audience like almost nothing else. So, a good principle to remember is this: avoid the appearance of evil.

Another principle that involves the Christian in the Christian community very clearly is influence. Three Scripture references address this question directly. In Romans 14, beginning with verse 7, Paul makes it clear that one of the major ways to decide right or wrong, particularly in issues that we don't have a chapter and verse for, is by how it is going to influence someone else: "None of us liveth to himself, and no man dieth to himself." Then in verse 10, "Why dost thou judge thy brother? or why dost thou set at nought thy brother?" And verse 12, "Every one of us shall give account of himself to God." That's a good thing to remember. Verse 13 adds, "Let us not therefore judge one another any more: but judge this rather, that no man put a stumblingblock or an occasion to fall in his brother's way." Verse 16, "Let not then your good be evil spoken of." So, something that is good for me might be evil to someone else. And then he gives this principle in verse 21: "It is good neither to eat flesh, nor to drink wine, nor any thing whereby thy brother stumbleth, or is offended, or is made weak."

In a discussion of this verse at a church meeting, someone said, "Then I wouldn't get out of bed in the morning." And someone else picked up on that and said, "If you stay in bed, that could cause some people to stumble too. So, you can't win either direction." Well, somewhere along the line there has to be some sanctified thinking in which God helps us with our logic. But influence is a principle that is clear in Paul's writing.

Let's go on to the second passage, where Paul is addressing the same question.

> But take heed lest by any means this liberty of yours become a stumblingblock to them that are weak. For if any man sees thee which hast knowledge sit at meat in the idol's temple, shall not the conscience of him which is weak be emboldened to eat those things which are offered to idols; and through thy knowledge shall the weak brother perish, for whom Christ died? But when ye sin so against the brethren, and wound their weak conscience, ye sin against Christ. Wherefore, if meat make my brother to offend, I will eat no flesh while the world standeth, lest I make my brother to offend (1 Corinthians 8:9-13).

The setting, of course, of these chapters is in the days of Paul. The pagans dedicated food, not only flesh, but all foods, to the idols. So, when they went to the marketplace (and sometimes the marketplaces were called "shambles"), they could buy food that had already been dedicated to the idols, and they had a head start on dinner that way, you see. So some of the Christians were buying foods that had been offered to idols, and others got into a big hassle over whether it was right to eat it or wrong to eat it. Paul basically said, "Big deal! Food offered to idols means nothing. Who cares? But if someone is offended, don't eat it."

And then he said something else rather interesting that sounds like talking out of both sides of his mouth. It is found in 1 Corinthians 10:23, 24. "All things are lawful for me, but all things are not expedient." Of course he says this within the limits of God's Word. Whatever God's Word doesn't condemn is lawful for me, but all things are not expedient. "All things are lawful for me, but all things edify not [or do not help]. Let no man seek his own, but every man another's wealth [or another's good]." And notice as he talks out of both sides of his mouth in verses 25, 28. "Whatsoever is sold in the shambles, that eat, asking no question. . . . *But if any man say unto you, This is offered in sacrifice unto idols, eat not* for his sake that shewed it" (emphasis supplied). So, if someone is going to be offended if you eat it, don't eat it. If someone is going to be offended if you don't eat it, then eat it, depending on whom you're with. Then he says in verse 32, "Give none offence, neither to the Jews, nor to the Gentiles, nor to the church of God" (not even with your necktie).

Apparently some things are not moral issues at all. So it makes no difference whether you do them or whether you don't. But they become moral issues when they offend someone else or cause someone to stumble.

During the days when churches had little to say about who their pastor would be, I was transferred to a new parish in Colorado and arrived completely unknown. I took my suit to the cleaners to be ready for Sabbath and went to the midweek meeting that Wednesday night. I sat in the back row and listened to the elder who was leading out in the meeting. After the prayer meeting he came to me and said, "Who are you, anyway?"

I said, "I am your new pastor."

"I thought so," he replied.

When I picked up my suit from the cleaners, it came back complete with a hanky in the pocket. Oh, I didn't usually wear a hanky in the pocket, but I thought it looked kind of nice, so I went ahead and preached my first Sabbath sermon in that church complete with the hanky. After the service was over, I was invited to a home for dinner—and the news was already out. There was a brother in that congregation who had passed the word up and down the aisle: "Watch out for this pastor! He'll leave the message. He'll go out in apostasy. He has a hanky in his pocket!"

When I heard that story, I decided I would put two hankies in my pocket the next week, or a big red one. But then I had to back up and say, Wait a minute! If I did that, then I would have just as big a problem as he does. Obviously he has a problem. I'm supposed to be his pastor, and I'd like to help him. I didn't need the hanky in the pocket. So, I made a summit decision that I would not wear a hanky in my pocket, at least not at that church.

I've told this story in the past, and people have told me afterward, "Oh, c'mon! Don't treat people so sick. If they've got a problem, let them own their problem. Don't go wishy-washy just because someone has that kind of a mentality." But that's not what Paul says. And here comes the test to your Christian brotherhood. Paul says, if you have weak people around who are going to stumble because of what you do, then don't do it. If you can get along without it, then don't do it. Isn't that the Bible principle?

Now, I'd like to be able to report to you that this man was converted from his ways and became a world spiritual leader of some kind. I can't. But I can tell you that we did become good friends, and we had many good talks. I was happy to pastor him, the best I knew how, without my hanky.

Would it be safe to consider this a principle for Christians:

If you can get along without something that might cause someone else to stumble, then go ahead and draw the line the other side of none. Is that fair? It seems to me that is what the Bible is saying.

But wait a minute! Is logic and reason or biblical rationale for what I do or don't do enough to solve all problems? Or is there a deeper solution to the problem of the gray area? I think there has to be. Isaiah 30:21 says, "Thine ears shall hear a word behind thee, saying, This is the way, walk ye in it." In John 10: 4, 5, Jesus essentially says, "My sheep hear my voice and follow me." John 16:13 says, The Holy Spirit "will guide you into all truth." Philippians 2:13 adds, "It is God which worketh in you both to will and to do of his good pleasure." Galatians 2:20 says, "I am crucified with Christ: nevertheless I live; yet not I, but Christ liveth in me."

Here we have something that is much bigger than simply asking the church or writing headquarters for answers. It has to do with a relationship with God by which we receive our own signals. Simply handling the question of right and wrong through logic and reason is inadequate. I am going to have to know how to receive signals from above.

In fact, I would like to propose, on the basis of this principle in Scripture, that the only person capable of even *discussing* right and wrong, let alone *knowing* right and wrong, is the person who has a vital relationship with Jesus day by day. That's the only way.

If, then, we should decide to have a group discussion about whether it is right to see the latest movie, then we should, in order to have a valid discussion, have two criteria: One, that the people who are coming to discuss it have seen the latest movie; two, that they also spend a significant time alone on their knees before God's Word day by day. Then we can have a meaningful discussion about right and wrong. Does that make sense?

But, even beyond that is the example of One who came on a long, expensive trip to save us.

In the early church, they used to baptize by immersion and wash feet at the Lord's Supper. Then someone said, "This is inconvenient. You get wet and you have to dry off. So why don't we do it a more convenient way?" And that's how all of the more convenient ways came along. However, I have never found in Scripture that we should do what we do on the basis of convenience. We should do it on the basis of what God says.

May I remind you that it was not convenient for Jesus to come and die. It wasn't convenient for Him to sweat drops of blood in the Garden of Gethsemane. When we look at Jesus, we don't see a middle-of-the-road moderate who is trying to get by with as little as He can. We don't even respect that attitude ourselves in medicine or education. When I go to a physician or a surgeon, I don't want someone who tried to get through with the lowest standards possible. I want someone who aimed at the top. Don't you?

That's why I would like to include this quotation that I think is dynamite. From *Steps to Christ*, page 45:

> Those who feel the constraining love of God, do not ask how little may be given to meet the requirements of God; they do not ask for the lowest standard, but aim at perfect conformity to the will of their Redeemer. With earnest desire they yield all and manifest an interest proportionate to the value of the object which they seek. A profession of Christ without this deep love is mere talk, dry formality, and heavy drudgery.

That makes sense to me. If I understand that I was born to live forever, and if I am only here on this earth for three score and ten years because God has something better, then I want to know all the principles of His kingdom. And I want Him to guide me to follow them, instead of trying to figure out how little I can get by with. Don't you agree?

So, please, in your mind's eye, catch the picture of the One who struggled in the garden and who made a decision to go ahead in spite of the sweat, in spite of the stress, to go through with it to save you and me. And picture yourself, in response to that love, giving your all to Him.

Chapter Five

Black, White, or Gray
Part Two

Someone once asked H. M. S. Richards, "Should women wear makeup?" He said, "When the barn needs painting, paint it." Although I am not exactly sure what all he meant by that, I wish our answers could be that simple.

But answers are seldom simple when we try to address the question of church standards and ethics. What is right and wrong? What do you do with the gray areas? The devil never takes a person from white to black in one big jump. He takes them through gray areas, little by little. And how do you know how to decide concerning right and wrong in gray areas such as where you go; what you eat; or what standards of music, entertainment, reading, television, and dress to choose?

To answer these questions, we must attempt to speak to principles. As a pastor, I find that people try to vacuum me into speaking about details, but I try to avoid them. You see, I used to have two teenage young people, a son with long hair and a daughter with short skirts. I had a problem because I wanted to influence them on both of those issues. But I knew that neither one of them had turned their lives over to Jesus yet. And I believe you can't make a religious issue out of church standards or personal ethics if a person hasn't turned his or her life over to Jesus yet. You just can't. If you do, you may push off their decision for Christ, because they see God stepping in and spoiling their lifestyle. So, I decided I'd have to be the goat and tell them what I wanted them to do. When they asked why, I replied, " Because I said so. That's all."

A lot of the rules and regulations at our schools don't have to have anything at all to do with God or faith or religion. And we can't try to make that the premise when we have many young people who haven't turned their lives over to Jesus yet. Once they have, and once they are in relationship with God, then it can make sense. But apart from that, no!

We know that in every congregation there are people who are listening but who haven't turned their lives over to Christ yet. So, we don't go into details and say things that might push them far away. That's why we speak to principles.

In pondering the importance of principle, I thought about the astronauts who train to go on the space shuttle. If I were an astronaut chosen for a mission, I wouldn't want to see how much I could get by with in the training program. I wouldn't want to see how little attention I could pay to the rules and standards of the trip and the training. I would want to aim at perfection. Wouldn't you? I'd want to have it down pat.

Now the inadvertent message that could come with this space illustration is that our standards and our rules and our regulations and our ethics have something to do with getting us from earth to heaven. So I want to back up and make this clear. When we talk about what's right and wrong and about ethics and morality, we're not talking about what gets us to heaven. We get to heaven only because of what Jesus did. Accepting that, and continuing to accept that through a daily relationship with Him until He comes, is the method of our salvation. On the other hand, my decisions concerning right and wrong and how I relate to my lifestyle in terms of all of these gray areas can have something to do with my relationship with Jesus.

I discovered that one night after staying up to watch the late, late show. It was a murder mystery, but I excused it because it had a missionary in it. It really made my *Desire of Ages* look boring the next morning. And that affected my devotional life. If whatever I am involved with, wherever I go, whatever I do, has an influence on my personal daily walk and relationship with Jesus, then it does have something to do with my journey from earth to heaven. Doesn't it?

Even the theologians of the new theology, who felt certain that justification is the gospel and that there is nothing more to the gospel, would add, sort of under their breath, "But God doesn't justify anybody that He doesn't also sanctify." So, when we talk about the standards of the church, or individual standards, when we talk about determining right from wrong, then we are addressing something that impacts our salvation, if it affects our relationship with Jesus.

So far we have given four principles by which to decide right and wrong:

Number one: What is my motive? Can I ask God to help me understand? What do I really want in this situation? (We usually have two reasons why we do what we do. A "good" reason and the real reason!)

Number two: Avoid the appearance of evil. This wouldn't make a whole lot of difference if we were marooned on a desert island. But we are in the world, where there are people, and even the appearance of evil brings dishonor to God's name.

Number three: The principle of influence. We haven't given enough credit to a little lady who wrote a lot of books discussing the power of influence. We think that this author was probably the most rigid, conservative, long-faced person around. But Ellen White hit the nail right on the head when it came to this. When we talk about certain standards, we have all kinds of surface reasons why we should or shouldn't. But to her, the main issue is influence. Don't do anything that would cause someone else to stumble or be offended, if it's something you don't need and you can get along without.

I punched the words *offended* and *offend* into my computer and discovered a text by the psalmist, one we've all heard one time or another: "Great peace have they which love thy law: and nothing shall offend them" (Psalm 119:165). I got a new insight into this old text. If someone in the church is offended by what I do, then they are proving that they don't love the law of God at all. They hate it.

So, if I do something that someone else thinks is wrong, because they are conservative, rigid defenders of God's law, and they get offended, this proves they don't love the law at all. Because "great peace have they which love the law: and nothing shall offend them." The truth is, they hate the law and are afraid, apparently, that I'm going to get away with something that they can't do.

Well, one reaction to those extreme kinds of people is, "Let them stew in their own juice." But Paul says, "No, don't offend even the people who hate the law and have been living on the nit-picking legalistic system all their lives." Paul said, Don't offend them. "Oh, but they have to own their own problem." "No! *I* own it too," he says. Don't offend them. And that's a Bible principle, because we're trying to help people move away from their problems toward something better.

Number four: What will it lead to? What other things are associated with it? Most of us are very familiar with this kind of story. We could give many illustrations of people who followed the downward path away from God. And most of us have experienced some of them.

Jesus prayed a beautiful prayer for those who live surrounded by paths that lead downward. Just before His arrest, during His time with His disciples, He said to His Father, "I pray not that thou shouldest take them out of the world, but that thou shouldest keep them from the evil" (John 17:15). We don't get up to the kind of standard that God has offered His children by becoming hermits or being marooned on a desert island. We don't get there by being flagpole sitters or by lying on beds of spikes. We are in the world. "I pray not that thou shouldest take them out of the world, but that thou shouldest keep them from the evil."

Our primary source for knowing what is right and wrong is our closeness to Jesus. With that in mind, I'd like to turn to the famous shepherd and sheep parable where Jesus is the shepherd and we are the sheep. Jesus is also the door to the sheepfold.

> Verily, verily, I say unto you, He that entereth not by the door into the sheepfold, but climbeth up some other way, the same is a thief and a robber. But he that entereth in by the door is the shepherd of the sheep. To him the porter openeth; and the sheep hear his voice; and he calleth his own sheep by name, and leadeth them out. And when he putteth forth his own sheep, he goeth before them, and the sheep follow him: *for they know his voice*. And a stranger will they not follow, but will flee from him: for they know not the voice of strangers (John 10:1-5, emphasis supplied).

The sheep follow Him, for they know His voice.

A man from Switzerland told me that when he was a boy, he and his neighbor friend would herd their sheep near each other on the mountainside. They had each other for company as they watched their sheep together. But, one day, a terrible storm blew in, and they had to run for shelter. The sheep scattered and got all mixed up together as they huddled in places of shelter during the thunder, lightning, wind, and rain.

When the storm was finally over, the shepherd boys were faced with trying to figure out whose sheep belonged to whom. They spent a long time trying to separate the sheep. Eventually, in frustration, they said, "We can't do it; we'll just have to go home and get help." So one boy headed one way, and the other boy headed the other way. To their surprise, the sheep separated themselves and followed their own shepherd. They knew their shepherd's voice, and they followed.

In the remarkable book *The Desire of Ages*, we find this statement: "When we know God as it is our privilege to know Him, our life will be a life of continual obedience" (page 668). Clearly, the emphasis is upon knowing God. But the very next paragraph speaks directly to our theme. "Those who decide to do nothing in any line that will displease God, will know, after presenting their case before Him, just what course to pursue. And they will receive not only wisdom, but strength."

So we have a sequence:

1. People know God one to one. (Back to relational theology again.)

2. They have a problem, trying to decide what's right or wrong.

3. They've determined that they're not going to displease God.

4. They are promised that they "will know, after presenting their case before Him, just what course to pursue."

5. They receive not only wisdom from above as to what is right and wrong in these gray areas, but they also receive power to do the right.

Isn't that good news? Many people have decided what is right but then couldn't follow it because they didn't have the power. If anyone thinks he's big enough to operate in terms of *knowing* right from wrong in the first place, and *doing* what is right in the second place, then he has a mistaken idea of who his God really is. We are not big enough to be God.

There are only two kinds of people in the world. Those who know God and those who don't know God. Both kinds of people are in every church, including my own. Both kinds of people are also outside of churches. Many people are disenchanted with organized religion today and want nothing to do with it, but they are still interested in God, and they are making efforts to know God through His Word and through prayer. Of these two kinds of people, surveys have demonstrated that it's only the minority in the Christian church who know God. The majority are still hooked on righteousness by heredity, righteousness by church membership, or righteousness by ethics or righteousness by celebration.

I'm going to risk another conclusion. I believe that when it comes to right and wrong, the people who know God are pretty much the same, wherever they are in the world. The same Holy Spirit is involved in their lives and in their relationship with God. He guides them in terms of right and wrong and provides the power to do right.

On the other hand, those who don't know God are like chameleons. They turn the color of whatever environment they happen to be in. (I suppose you've heard of the chameleon that got on the Scottish plaid and went stark raving crazy!) It can really drive you up the wall if you are going to decide what's right and wrong simply on the basis of the crowd you're with. But that's how it works for the people who don't know God. To them, religion and church is nothing more than a club, and they conform to the norm of that club, whatever the norm may be.

A pastoral call took us to southern California from the Northwest one time, and we were concerned about moving to southern California. We had heard a lot about those "southern California Adventists." During the time that I pastored at the White Memorial Church, it was interesting to observe some of the students who arrived at Loma Linda University from back East, the conservative back East. They were conservative when they arrived. But they changed almost overnight. They conformed to the atmosphere they found themselves in. It was so obvious, you couldn't miss it. And it gave evidence that their standards, their ethics, their lifestyle, were simply determined by the crowd they were in.

Isn't there something deeper driving us? There should be. I don't want my decisions concerning right and wrong to be influenced or decided by the crowd I am with.

Years ago, during my first year in the ministry, I worked in a little town near Bakersfield, California. I was supposed to be responsible for Taft, a town out there beyond the oil fields. There, a little churchful of people were zealous to share their belief with others. So we began some Bible studies, and people came. I probably gave more Bible studies that first year than any year since.

It was fascinating to watch people who seemed interested in the gospel. One young couple just couldn't get enough in one study. They would say, "Come and study another time with us. Come over after church and eat with us, and let's study some more." We studied the Bible with them every chance we had. Their appetite was unquenchable.

However, when it came to appearances, the young woman looked like the scarlet beast and the woman of Revelation 17. She was overdone, even for the world, with half a dozen chokers, earrings down to the shoulders, and bracelets all the way up the arm. I mean it was really something, complete with dark purple makeup! We never did talk about her makeup and jewelry. All we did was study the Bible.

And as I watched, "the painting of the barn" began to change. I got nervous. I really got nervous about it! I decided that some legalistic church member next door must be working them over. But, gradually it happened. The purple changed to red and then to pink. The chokers went from six to five to four, down to one, and then none. The earrings down to the shoulder got shorter and shorter. She must have had a terrific collection of jewelry somewhere. But all these things began to drop off.

I continued to be nervous about it, especially when I arrived one day and found them both chewing on pieces of wood. I thought they were losing their minds! "What are you doing?" I asked.

"We're trying to quit smoking."

"Why? Why are you trying to quit smoking? Has someone been talking to you about it?"

"No."

"Then why all of these changes in your lifestyle?"

"We don't know."

There was simply a principle at work. As Jesus came in, they changed spontaneously. I can't tell you how many times I've seen this happen as people got into the Bible and began to think of the things of heaven. As Jesus comes in, we find the only real answer to right and wrong.

It may be different for various individuals at different stages in their lives. We need to allow for that and not try to look into each other's closets and refrigerators. But it still happens, and it's real. Because those who know God are being led to a life of continual obedience. They know, as they spend time with Him, just which course to pursue. They receive wisdom and power as well.

What conclusion can we draw from all of this? Genuine sheep know the Shepherd's voice. He has a way of communicating His will to them at any particular time and under any circumstances. I can't explain it. You can't explain it. But we can experience it. And the closer we come to Jesus, the more certainty we have in determining right or wrong for ourselves, under the circumstances we are in at that time.

There is this significant text from the apostle Paul, Hebrews 12:1, 2: "Seeing we also are compassed about with so great a cloud of witnesses, let us lay aside every 'sin'." Do you remember what the word is? "Let us lay aside every *weight*." The weight may not be a sin, but it's a weight. It's something that holds back our relationship with Christ. "Let us lay aside every weight, *and* the sin which doth so easily beset us, and let us run with patience the race that is set before us, looking unto Jesus" (emphasis supplied). And when we look unto Jesus, the sins and the weights are affected. They get left behind.

I have a question for you. It is based upon personal experiences with people who are facing crises in their lives—tragedy, sorrow, terminal illness, or loss of a loved one. Have you ever noticed that there are some things, gray-area rights and wrongs, that somehow don't seem so important in the face of tragedy and crisis? Have you experienced this? Somehow, in those times, we can better see what is really important and what is peripheral.

But, I'd like to ask you, if you knew for certain that Jesus was going to return in six months, would that have any effect on where you go, what you do, or your lifestyle, particularly in the gray areas? Would it? Honestly? I think so. Maybe that's not a bad question to ask ourselves.

Are there going to be any "squeeze plays" at the pearly gates of the city of God? Are we going to rush in with the very minimum standard and try to get through the gates into the heavenly country?

Back in the early days of the West, a stagecoach company had an opening for a driver. The company invited people to apply, and three men responded. As the first one was interviewed, he was asked, "Do you know that particular dangerous spot on the mountain road where the precipice goes straight down on one side and the rock wall straight up on the other? How close can you come to the edge and make it safely through?"

He said, "I have had a lot of experience. I can drive within a foot of the edge and make it safely through."

They interviewed the second stagecoach driver. Again they asked, "Do you know that place . . . ? How close can you come to the edge and still make it though?"

He said, "I have had a lot of experience. I know my driving. I know my horses. I can drive within six inches of the edge and make it safely through."

They called the third man in, and he said, "I don't know how close I can come to the edge and make it through. But I'll tell you one thing, I am going to stay as far from the edge as I can." He got the job!

I told that story at church one time, and a church member came to me afterward and said, "I have been driving so far from the edge for the last umpteen years that I 'wiped out' banging against the rock wall on the other side." I guess that happens too, but the basic truth still holds. Do you really want to live in heaven with people who have tried to get by with as much as possible before they got there?

Perhaps we can see Jesus again, reflected on the plains of Dura. In the eyes of those three Hebrew men, Shadrach, Meshach, and "To-bed-we-go." (That's what my boy called him, because when that story ended, it was bedtime.) I can still remember as a little child myself, listening to my uncle preach about these three Hebrew worthies. They had spoiled the party that day. Nebuchadnezzar wanted to make sure that there would be no Medo-Persia, Greece, and Rome. So, he had this huge image erected. Everybody was supposed to bow down when they heard the music.

Suddenly a messenger came running to Nebuchadnezzar and said, "There are three who did not bow down." So he called them into his presence. He recognized them as his friends. He had a lot of respect for them.

Perhaps his plea went something like this: "Oh, c'mon, fellows. I know about you. I know about your God. And I have a lot of sympathy for what you believe in. I really admire you. But we're trying to do something here today for the sake of the nation, the kingdom. Go ahead and pray to your own God. Just get down on one knee, maybe. Just get down on one knee and look the other way. You don't have to look at the image. Have a little prayer to your God. Just don't spoil the party. Whatever you do, just don't spoil the party."

And you remember what they said. "O Nebuchadnezzar, we are not careful to answer you in this matter. We will not bow down" (see Daniel 3:16-18). They were not middle-of-the-road moderates. They were people who were dedicated to the God whom they served. And nothing would swerve them from obedience to Him. As the Spirit of God speaks to you, I'd like to invite you to decide in your own mind that you're not going to aim at the least or the most you can get by with. Aim at the highest standard.

Chapter
Six

Situation Ethics

I f someone tried to break into my house and harm my family, I would fight to the death." That was a statement made to us by my theology professor in college. Later, as a pastor, I visited two little old ladies who lived next door to each other. All three of us were together at one of their homes, when we got into the question of security and what would happen if someone tried to break in. One of the little ladies said, "I'd just have to trust the Lord." The other lady said, "I have a pistol under the bedsprings. It's loaded, and the safety is off." I looked at her trembling hand and thought, "C'mon, Grandma, shaking like that, you'd have trouble hitting the wall!"

As we address this issue of standards, this short stack of hot cakes on the Adventist scene, I am taking the position that the religion of Jesus Christ in the heart does not lead us to a lower standard in life; it leads us to the highest we've ever known. It doesn't make me less of a Seventh-day Adventist; it makes me more of a Seventh-day Adventist. Love, forgiveness, and acceptance do not do away with standards in the life; they improve the lifestyle on the side of God. This doesn't mean that all the women start wearing their hair in a bun and putting on square heels, and all the men begin wearing as much black as they can and putting on long faces. It does do away with some of our traditions. But, it certainly doesn't drag the standard of Christian living in the dust. If it does, it isn't the religion of Jesus Christ at all. So I am defending the ethics and morality that the Bible teaches.

In this chapter we're going to take a look at situation ethics, the new morality of recent years. It is showing its face again. In fact, you've probably heard about it from television, the newspaper, and the news magazines. Mainline denominations are examining their standards, and some of them are trying to "go with the flow." Others are resisting the flow and trying to stand firm. There is a new term for this type of ethics: "justice-love." And there is an ongoing debate about where it will lead us.

Is it all right to do the wrong thing if you do it for the right reason? That's the idea behind the new approach. Is that idea biblical? Is it OK as long as love is the motive?

Some people, who like to think in modern ways, think the Ten Commandments are sort of legalistic, sort of old hat. But the question is, when it comes to the Christian faith, do we go by what the Bible says, or do we go by what we think?

I can remember hearing an old-time evangelistic sermon on the sawdust trail, which was simply titled, "God says, but I think . . ." I didn't even have to listen to the sermon. The title said it all. God says, but I think. Are we interested in what God says? Or are we simply interested in what we think? Are we going to be our own God?

In our discussion of standards, we've found that one principle that helps us understand how to decide is our *influence*. As you've noticed, we're trying to stay away from the details and simply speak to the principles of standards and ethics. And influence is one of the big ones. We've studied it in the apostle Paul's writings. Even though something appears not to be a moral issue at all, it becomes a moral issue (and thus becomes immoral), at whatever point it causes someone else to be wrongly influenced or to be offended or to stumble.

"Oh, but I think that's being too sensitive to other people's sick minds."

"No, that's what God says."

"But I think that we are catering to the childish people."

"What matters is what God's Word says, not what we think."

As we take a look at situation ethics, we're going to try to analyze the deliberate breaking of God's law—for the right reason. Take a woman, for instance, who has a terminal illness. She has always been concerned about other people. Now she feels that she has become a burden on others and would like to shorten her own life out of love for other people who have to take care of her. Is that all right? Is anything wrong with that? Is it the loving thing to do?

What about the Desert Storm conflict over in the Middle East? Some suggested that the problem was Iraq's leader, so he should be "surgically" removed. It wouldn't cost that much, either, to hire the hit man to do it. Would that be all right for the purpose of saving thousands and thousands of people's lives? Is it the right thing to do because it's the loving thing, even though it's the wrong thing?

What about Joseph Fletcher's classic examples at the end of his book about situation ethics? After he outlines the new morality, he gives some case histories to sharpen the reader's new morality fangs on. Perhaps you recall the case of Mrs. Burgemyer:

As the Russian armies drove westward to meet the Americans and British at the Elbe, a Soviet patrol picked up a Mrs. Burgemyer foraging for food for her three children. Unable to even get word to the children, and without any clear reason for it, she was taken off to a prison camp in the Ukraine. Her husband had been captured in the war and had been taken to a P.O.W. camp in Wales. When he was returned to Berlin, he spent weeks and weeks rounding up his three children. Then Mother's whereabouts became crucial. They never stopped searching. She, more than anything, was needed to reknit

71

them as a family in that dire situation of hunger, chaos, and fear. In the Ukraine, Mrs. Burgemyer learned, through a sympathetic commandant, that her husband and the family were trying to keep together and were looking for her. But the rules allowed them to release her for only two reasons. One, illness, requiring medical facilities beyond the camp, for which she would be transferred to a Soviet hospital farther back, and two, pregnancy, in which case she would be returned to Germany as a liability.

She turned things over in her mind and finally asked a friendly Volga German camp guard to help her out. Which he did. When pregnancy was medically verified, she was sent back to Berlin and to her family. They welcomed her with open arms, even when she told them how she had managed it. When the child was born, they loved him more than all the rest, in the view that little Deitrich had done more for them than anybody else.

When it was time for him to be christened, they took him to the pastor on a Sunday afternoon. After the ceremony, the parents sent Deitrich home with the other children and sat down in the pastor's study to ask him whether they were right to feel as they did about Mrs. Burgemyer and Deitrich. Should they be grateful to the Volga German guard? Had Mrs. Burgemyer done a good and right thing?

I tried this story out on one congregation a number of years ago. Several ladies, during the potluck after church, discussed the story and agreed that Mrs. Burgemyer had done a very clever and wonderful thing. They also hoped that if they had been in the same situation, they could have thought of something as good and as clever.

Fritz Ridenour discussed this same story in his book *It All Depends*, in which he challenges and criticizes the new morality. He brings up some other facets of the story, which go something like this: Despite the fact that Mrs. Burgemyer's purpose was certainly very noble, she cunningly exploited a fellow human being to serve her purpose. Would situation ethicists really believe that she treated the guard as a person? Did he have a family? In her concern for her own family, Mrs.

Burgemyer lost sight of love's interest for him. Somehow, when we go across God's set of rules, someone always gets hurt.

This critic of the new morality came up with a few extra chapters to the story, which go something like this: Suppose the woman has become pregnant by the guard and is now free, but is still two hundred miles away from home, and it is winter. Unless she gets food soon, she will starve to death, and her original act of "sacrificial adultery" will have been in vain. So she comes to a farmhouse, and the farmer offers her food if she will . . . yes, you guessed it.

Well, if the woman was right to become involved with the guard, it follows that in this situation, since she is desperate for food, it is only right that she should submit to the farmer. So, she does and gets food. Once again, she finds herself out on the road and discovers that she can't walk the rest of the way home. She is tired, and she will probably freeze to death. A truck driver comes along and offers her a ride, if . . . Certainly if her act with the guard was right and also with the farmer, why not the trucker?

So, she finally gets back to a city near the village where her children are. But, suppose the husband has no adequate way to support the children. It is hardly practical to be reunited with her children and then to lovingly starve to death with them. But, there are enough men in the city who are also interested in using this woman that she is soon able to raise a sizable bankroll. In fact, the size of her bankroll convinces her that by accumulating still greater funds, she can demonstrate even more love for her children and provide for them in an even better way.

Fritz Ridenour admits that the story has now gotten to absurd proportions. But then he asks the question, "At what point did the story become absurd?" Not a bad question.

So, you are faced today, just as yesteryear, with the question, Is it all right to do the wrong thing for the right reason? Or is somebody always going to get hurt? And did God give us the ten rules just to make it tough on us or because He knows the machinery by which we run? God's laws can be looked at, not as restrictions, but as instructions. If you have something that you want to operate correctly, check the instructions, and they will reveal the proper course of action.

I had a preacher friend whose wife became discouraged whenever she tried to sew. She never seemed to be able to satisfactorily complete a garment.

He said, "Are you following the instructions?"

"Well, I am trying to."

He said, "Give me the fabric and the pattern, and I will make a dress."

He followed the instructions meticulously and made a beautiful dress.

I tried to cross the Mojave Desert with the "freedom" of not having changed the antifreeze in my Honda for several years. I never read the instructions. The aluminum heads eroded, the head gasket blew, and my freedom of not having to change my antifreeze led to my loss of freedom as I sat by the side of the road in the desert.

When in doubt, check the instruction book! It's not restriction, it's revelation. It isn't, "Oh, must I do this?" It is, "Isn't it wonderful to know?" The moment you do away with rules, you are destroying yourself. You can't even have a game without rules. It is a wonderful thing to know where you belong. If you don't, you will never rest until you find out.

A university president told me that any child's security is directly in proportion to the predictability of his parents. And any human being's security is in direct proportion to the predictability of his God, the One who made him. Human beings are free to choose for or against God's law. But, if they make their choice against it, then sooner or later, one way or another, they lose their freedom. That's just the way it is.

If there is anything we ought to know today, it's relational theology rather than simply behavioral theology. The very principle of salvation by faith is against trying to save yourself. It is trusting God for your salvation. And why shouldn't this apply when it comes to the Ukraine, the prison camp, or the slow death? In fact, as you study the rationale behind the standards and ethics that our church has been known for, once again, I am pleased to remind you that Ellen White gets pretty good marks for hitting the target.

I want to quote a sample from that book on the life of Christ, *The Desire of Ages*. In the chapter that talks about Jesus in the wilderness, He is struggling with a problem. He is hungry. He needs relief. But what does He do? He waits God's time to bring relief and food. He is in the wilderness in obedience to God, and He will not obtain food by following the suggestions of Satan. He testifies that it is a lesser calamity to suffer, whatever may befall, than to depart in any manner from the will of God.

> Perhaps it appears that obedience to some plain requirement of God will cut off his means of support. Satan would make him believe that he must sacrifice his conscientious convictions. But the only thing in our world upon which we can rely is the word of God. "Seek ye first the kingdom of God, and His righteousness; and all these things shall be added unto you." Matthew 6:33. Even in this life it is not for our good to depart from the will of our Father in heaven. When we learn the power of His word, we shall not follow the suggestions of Satan in order to obtain food or to save our lives. Our only question will be, What is God's command? and what is His promise? Knowing these, we shall obey the one, and trust the other (p. 121).

Does that sound risky? Does it sound dangerous? Does it sound right?

Perhaps you remember John Weidner, the Christian who helped more than a thousand Jews escape to freedom during World War II. Finally he was captured and put in prison. He was scheduled to be executed the next day. As he sat in prison, he began to think about the Bible. He thought about the three Hebrew worthies and their deliverance from the fiery furnace, and he took courage. He thought about Daniel and his deliverance from the lions' den, and he felt better. Then he thought about John the Baptist, and he began working to break out of the prison What did he think? What do we think?

What is God's command? and what is His promise? Has God always promised to deliver? No. Read the last part of Hebrews 11. There we find that some were sawn asunder, and some were tortured. These all died in faith, not having received the promise of His coming. But they died in faith. Do I trust Him, whether I live or die? Do I know Him enough to trust Him? Do I trust Him enough to know that I am in my present circumstances because He led me here?

Can I trust Him, even unto death? That's the question. Wasn't He the One who said, Don't be afraid of the ones who kill the body, be afraid of those who kill the soul (see Matthew 10:28)?

Huss and Jerome died with green wood fueling a slowly burning fire. Their ashes were tossed into the Rhine, but the persecutors never got close to their souls.

So is it ever the right thing to do wrong for a loving reason? The principle that we introduce here to answer that question covers a lot of ground. It is simply this: where is my trust? Is it in what I can do, in how clever I can be? Or is my trust in God and what He sees best? This principle covers a lot of ethical and moral decisions that we are faced with today.

One Sabbath after we talked about these principles in church, some commented, "We can appreciate that you've been talking about principles, and not details."

Then one woman added, "Yes, but for the first time I understand why I should question wearing my wedding ring."

I said, "I never mentioned it."

"I know, I know," she said, "you never mentioned it. But the principles apply."

What about the principles in our institutions? What about right or wrong, when it comes to the standards of the church? What about standards for church leadership? What about the nominating committees? What are they going to look at? Is it nit-picking and legalistic to elect church leaders who don't want to offend others by the things they do?

Recently, in a book called *Set Free*, the author gave his typical, all-traditional list of being clean. He called it being squeaky clean. "No shining shoes on Sabbath, no flesh foods, no baths after sunset, no mixed bathing, no baking on Sabbath, no coffee or tea, no eating between meals, no wedding rings, no dancing, no chess or checkers, no card playing, no bowling, no catsup or mustard, no pepper, no alcohol beverages, no television, no tennis, no fruits and vegetables at the same meal, no ice cream, no cheese and no life insurance."

I read this list in church one day, and a little boy said to his dad, "That's sick. But," he added, "I can go along with no vegetables!"

Can you go along with anything on the list? If so, on what basis? Do any of the principles apply here? What about the simpler days, when our church used to say, "Look, on things you don't really need, draw the line on the other side of none." Today, we have tried to draw the line in a different place on many things, and as a result, we get into these endless hassles of *where* to draw the line. There is always the constant trend downward. Isn't that true? Have you noticed it? It's always there. The trend is never upward, but always downward.

Back in the old days, when we drew the line the other side of none, people would say, "They are treating us like imbeciles! Can't we think for ourselves?"

Which is the best way for deciding church standards? In some areas, we probably should be allowed to think it through. But how? What is the ultimate answer when we get into these sticky questions? How are we going to decide?

To answer these questions, let's consider this text:

> If ye then be risen with Christ [What does that mean? I have been buried with Him by baptism. I rise again to walk in newness of life.], seek those things which are above, where Christ sitteth on the right hand of God. Set your affection on things above, not on things on the earth. For ye are dead, and your life is hid with Christ in God. When Christ, who is our life, shall appear, then shall ye also appear with him in glory. Mortify therefore your members which are upon the earth (Colossians 3:1-5).

A more modern translation says, "Away then with sinful,

earthly things; deaden the evil desires lurking within you" (TLB). We can't do that. Only God can.

In spite of all our logic and reason, we have to come to this major premise: the ultimate answer in all situations is knowing God as our personal friend, knowing Jesus and His voice.

In 1 John 2:15-17, we hear Jesus calling us to the upward look, instead of to the inward and the outward look. "Love not the world." Well, how are you going to interpret that? Don't drive a car? Don't wear a watch? Don't buy a refrigerator because that's of the world? What does it mean to love not the world, "neither the things that are in the world"? Is it wrong to want to have a new car?

> If any man love the world, the love of the Father is not in him. For all that is in the world, the lust of the flesh, and the lust of the eyes, and the pride of life, is not of the Father, but is of the world. And the world passeth away, and the lust thereof: but he that doeth the will of God abideth for ever.

What does it mean when it says, "If any man love the world, the love of the Father is not in him"?

What does it mean to love the world to that extent? And what does "the lust of the flesh, and the lust of the eyes, and the pride of life" mean? Here is the more modern translation, "These are the evil things in the world, number one, wanting things to please our sinful self. Number two, wanting the sinful things we see. Number three, being too proud of the things we have."

The idea of fasting provides us with a good illustration. When Jesus came down from the mount of transfiguration, the disciples had been defeated. They couldn't cast a devil out of a boy. But Jesus did. When it was all over, Jesus said, "This kind cometh not out except by prayer and fasting" (see Matthew 17:21). There is no evidence that Jesus had been fasting. As far as we know, He hadn't been fasting. So, what does it mean to fast? This must be referring to an *attitude* of fasting, a state of mind that qualifies for fasting. May I suggest that it means this: If I have to make a choice between eating and time alone with God, I already know what the choice will be. If I have to make that kind of choice, I would choose time with God. That is what real fasting means.

Now, let's apply that idea to "love not the world." I can turn that into a legalistic checklist that will make me a hermit or a monk. Or I can see the issue to be that, whatever I would choose before God and before my relationship with Him has to go; that, if I know Jesus as my personal Friend and Saviour, nothing is going to take priority above that relationship. Is it wrong for me to want a new car so my old one doesn't leave me on the side of the road in the desert? No, but if I have to have a new car that in some way militates against my personal fellowship with Jesus, then I have neglected the warning of 1 John 2. Where will your choice come? Where will my choice be when it comes to my love for God and my relationship with Him? That's the important question.

Now let's lift aside the veil and look once again at the bigger picture. If you knew that Jesus was coming back next week, just what would be your lifestyle? What would you do? Where would you go? How would you dress? What would you eat, and what would you drink? What kind of entertainment would you choose? Is that a fair question? "Oh," you say, "that's a fearful question." No, not if He's your friend.

C. S. Lewis says it rather interestingly:

> I do not find that pictures of physical catastrophes, signs in the cloud, heaven rolled up like a scroll, help one so much as the naked idea of judgment. We cannot always be excited. We can perhaps train ourselves to ask, more and more often, how the thing which we are saying or doing or failing to do at each moment will look when the irresistible light streams in upon it—that light which is so different from the light of this world. And yet even now we know just enough of it to take it into account. Women sometimes have the problem of trying to judge by artificial light how a dress would look by daylight. That is very like the problem of all of us, to dress our souls, not for the electric lights of the present world, but for the

daylight of the next. The good dress is the one that will face that light, for that light will last forever.

But is that Light a friendly presence or an unfriendly presence? It all depends on whether you know Him. If you have gotten acquainted with Him, you know He is your best friend. And who doesn't want to please his or her best friend? And then comes the big surprise—to discover that this best friend knew all along what was best for us.

Sometimes we fool ourselves into believing that we know what is best for us. And when we do, Jesus must weep at the pain we insist on inflicting on ourselves. Too often, we think like the woman in this story.

Bye-Bye, Rabboni

"And Jesus said, 'Neither do I condemn you; go and do not sin again.' "

The woman rose from her frightened crouch and started to scurry away. But then, as though suddenly aware of Jesus' closing injunction, she stopped and looked quizzically at her rescuer.

"What do you mean, 'Do not sin again'?" she asked.

"I think you know what I mean," Jesus replied.

"But I don't know, Rabbi. Unless you are suggesting that my relationship with Reuben is sinful."

"What would you call it?"

"A significant relationship," the woman answered. "An interpersonal commitment in which each of us seeks to realize our full potential."

"Oh, really!" Jesus said.

"Reuben and I love one another. Surely you know what that means. How can a relationship be sinful when it expresses true love?"

"But what about your covenant with your husband?"

"Isaac? Well, Rabbi, Isaac and I have never really turned one another on. We cannot realize our full sexuality together."

"What does that have to do with . . . ?"

"Come now, Rabboni, people have a duty to themselves, you

know, a right to their happiness."

"They do?"

"Certainly! Why should we let outmoded legalism tie us into relationships that are sterile and unfulfilling?"

"Oh, you mean that Isaac is unable to father children; and you hope that Reuben . . . ?"

"Rabbi, you're putting me on. You know very well what I mean. God knows, Isaac can father children. I have three of them to prove that."

"You have three children, and you propose to ignore your marriage vows and carry on with this man Reuben?"

"O Rabbi, you're really cute! 'Carry on with this man Reuben.' That kind of talk went out with the age of the judges. I'm not saying that Reuben and I will stay together forever. We may very well outgrow one another after a time and need room to explore our authentic selfhoods. People do change, you know."

"But the children?"

"Kids aren't as fragile as you think, Rabboni. You'd be surprised at how well they get along with Reuben, the way they hang on him when he stays for breakfast. When Isaac is away on a camel drive, that is. They call him 'Uncle Rube,' and he does magic tricks for them—and they like that. They much prefer him to Nathan."

"Nathan?"

"My previous significant relationship. He got to be a terrible bore. Said his conscience bothered him and legalistic stuff like that. I told him he should pay more attention to people like you."

"Like me? How might I have helped him?"

"Oh, you know. That stuff you say about not being paralyzed by guilt and fearing human opinion?"

"Ah, yes. That. But tell me, if this Reuben loves you so deeply, why wasn't he here today?"

"He wanted to be, Rabbi. He really did. Very much. But he just can't stand the sight of blood. He's a very sensitive person. Not at all like Joshua."

"Joshua? Another significant . . . ?"

81

"Oh, that was over long ago. And it wasn't really significant. Not really. You might say I was just trying my wings."

"And then again, I might not."

"Mmmmmmmmm?"

"What will you say to your husband about today?"

"I'll tell him to view it as a learning experience, a chance to broaden his horizons. Well, I must run now. Bye-bye, Rabboni. Have a good day."

Jesus gazed reflectively after the departing figure. Then he stared at the ground and the tears began to fall . . . and fall . . . and fall.[1]

---

1. *Insight,* 10 November 1963.

Chapter
Seven

Sleeping in Class

We must have slept through some classes. We didn't even realize until later that we had. I'm not talking about general psychology, right after lunch, where my brother and I bought one textbook and one notebook—so he could sleep one day while I took notes and trade off the next day. I'm talking about some other classes in college that I must have slept through. And, of all things, they had to do with the only answer to life's biggest questions—knowing Jesus as my best friend.

If we look in the book of Romans, we find a strong invitation to not sleep, to wake up, particularly in the time in which we live.

> Knowing the time, that now it is high time to awake out of sleep: for now is our salvation nearer than when we believed [or first believed]. The night is far spent, the day is at hand: let us therefore cast off the works of darkness, and let us put on the armor of light. Let us

walk honestly, as in the day; not in rioting and drunkenness, not in chambering and wantonness, not in strife and envying. But *put ye on the Lord Jesus Christ*, and make not provision for the flesh, to fulfill the lusts thereof (Romans 13:11-14, emphasis supplied).

This scripture has something to do with putting on the Lord Jesus Christ, a truth that I slept through. Many of us spend more time and effort trying to not make "provision for the flesh." We spend more time concentrating on our failures, our weaknesses, and our sins than we do putting on the Lord Jesus Christ. Sometimes we have spent more time on church rules and standards, or, lately, on getting rid of them, than on knowing Him.

A preacher friend of mine, who went through college about the same time I did, was later called to the bedside of a dying man. There was one thing that this sick man wanted to know: "How can I know that I am right with God?"

My friend told me of his own frustration. The dying man didn't ask him to conjugate some Greek verbs. He didn't ask him to rattle off a few key texts proving certain church teachings. He didn't ask him to diagram sentences or to recite some well-known verses from the literary greats. He didn't ask him about morality or Christian ethics or anything else except the one class that my friend had slept through. How can I know that I am right with God?

When I heard that, I said, "I slept through that one too." Trying to be fair to the faculty, my friend said, "It must have been taught there somewhere, but I must have been sleeping."

I feel that many of us slept through the classes that taught answers to the really heavy questions people are asking. Part of the problem is that we can accept certain things in theory and sleep through them in experience. From the earliest days I can remember, I have understood that Jesus was important, but I haven't always felt that Jesus was that important in terms of experience. Can there be a gap there? Can there be a difference?

Our church has always believed theoretically in the tenet or doctrine of salvation through faith in Christ alone. When

Elder Richards was asked one day what the Adventist message is, he replied, "Jesus only." I like that. But has that been your experience during your exposure to Adventism?

Do people think of Seventh-day Adventists as people who preach and teach and live "Jesus only," or do they think of them as people who don't eat pork and who go to church on Saturday instead of Sunday? We have never been asleep on the doctrinal belief in Jesus when it comes to the back of our baptismal certificate. But is it possible to be asleep experientially?

The disciples were followers of Jesus. But one has to admit that even though they had forsaken their nets, they didn't forsake the ground they were sleeping on in Gethsemane. They followed Jesus all the way to Gethsemane. Then, as recorded in Luke 22:46, He came to them and said, "Why sleep ye? Rise and pray, lest ye enter into temptation."

I hope that somewhere along the line, everyone will hear the voice of the Holy Spirit in the morning saying, "Why sleep ye? Rise and pray."

Some of us have made a study of the young people in our particular subculture. It appears that as a rule, before about the junior year in the academy, most Adventist young people don't even know what you're talking about when you talk about salvation by faith in Jesus only and the deeper life of relationship, not just religion. (There are exceptions to the rule, and there is evidence that this perimeter is being pushed further back all the time. Praise God for that!)

As a rule, the most fertile time for a young person, in our subculture, to find something more than "religion" and begin the deeper life with God might be somewhere between the years of grades eleven through fourteen—the last two years of high school and the first two years of college. If you happen to be in that category, keep awake. Don't close your eyes. There is something very important for you to understand, so don't risk sleeping through it.

If you don't find the deeper life with Jesus at this time, something more than "Jesus loves me, this I know" (which might have been great when you were four and five years old), something more than just religion and formal routine, then it might take years and years before you do. Because you will inevitably get involved in the two other major decisions of life: who you're going to spend your life with and what your vocation will be.

Somehow, the relationship with God, the most important decision, gets pushed back into the corner. In the meantime, while it's in the corner, there will be heartaches, stress, tragedy, sleepless nights, and confusion until, finally, you wake up to the class that you slept through.

We know that many people are sick and tired of organized religion. ("Tired of religion—why not try Jesus?") And some young people attend Christian schools against their own choice. But when your folks offer you a new sports car if you go to school at their alma mater, how can you refuse? How could a young person turn down an offer to have his or her tuition paid and other financial needs met?

I've even heard of kids who were offered a new motorcycle for getting baptized! Some young people see the fallacy of that kind of thinking. They don't have any interest in religion because it didn't do that much for their parents.

I'd like to offer you something more than religion, because there's a big difference between being religious and being spiritual, between knowing the rules, the standards, and the doctrines and knowing the Lord. And if you haven't seen that difference yet, don't sleep through it. Some of us did, and we got ulcers in the process.

The first class I slept through in college was the one on sin. I don't mean that they had a course 101 AB, Sin. But somewhere along the line, I missed the lesson on what sin is all about. I had the idea that sin is doing bad things. And I wasn't doing that much bad in full view. Most of us were victims of righteousness by training, righteousness by habit, righteousness by inhibition. We were scared to do anything bad. We were "good livers" on the outside. And, of course, if you're a good liver, then you're not a victim of doing bad things as a rule, and, therefore, you're not a sinner. Right? Wrong!

The age-old definition of sin quoted from Scripture, the one we always get when we ask for it—"Sin is the transgression of the law"—is not enough, at least in the way it is commonly understood. What it really says is, "Whosoever committeth sin transgresseth *also* the law" (1 John 3:4, emphasis supplied). There's something deeper in the issue of sin. One has to commit "sin" first before he can break the law in the way we usually think. Sin *results* in breaking the law. To my surprise, I slept through that one. I didn't find out until several years later that sin is living a life apart from God, day by day (which is really breaking the first commandment by becoming my own god).

Jesus said it in John 16:8, referring to the Holy Spirit's work. "When he is come, he will reprove the world of sin." In verse 9, He defines sin as not believing in the Lord Jesus. But believing, by itself, is not enough, and the proof is that "the devils also believe, and tremble" (James 2:19). A better word would be *trust*.

Sin is "not trusting in Jesus." That definition immediately suggests a relationship, a close relationship of dependence upon Him.

Romans 14:23 says the same thing using different words. "Whatsoever is not of faith is sin." So anything I do—studying religion classes, studying mathematics, studying health, studying chemistry or nursing, or even doing good deeds and holding high standards—if I am living a life apart from a meaningful relationship with the Lord Jesus, is living in sin. I slept through that class.

There's a big difference between *sin* and *sins*. *Sin* is living a life apart from Jesus, and this results in *sins*, or doing bad things.

Most of us who have a problem with sins work harder on the sins than we do on the effort toward the relationship with Jesus. What an awakening it was when I got that straight! But forming a relationship with Jesus must be more than just a theory. It must be an experience as well.

The second class I slept through was the one on righteousness. Again, there wasn't an upper-division class called Righteousness 450 AB. But I missed it. I thought that righteousness was doing what is right. In fact, I heard people define it that way. Whenever the question "What is righteousness?" was asked, the answer always came, "Righteousness is right doing." We even had quotes to prove it. But, if there's nothing more to righteousness than right doing, then all we have to do is do what's right, and we will be righteous. Look at the trap this leads us into! If we know the least thing about salvation, we know that definition is wrong. And, of course, most of us who were doing pretty well, as far as people could see, never considered our thoughts or our desires to be a problem. So we didn't need God. If we're doing what's right, and we are not getting kicked out of school, if we haven't burned the dormitory down, and we've gotten rid of all of our rock records, then who needs God? God needs to take care of the bad people, we know. But do the good people even need God?

On the other hand, how do you define right and wrong in the climate of new morality and situation ethics? Some Christians believe it is wrong to drink wine, and others think it's good for you. We can list all kinds of issues like this, as suggested in earlier chapters. Without Jesus Christ, all of us define right doing on the basis of our training, habits, and the inhibitions that have been built into us. Isn't that right?

On the basis of the difference in training and background, we have as many different opinions as we have people. It is impossible to understand right and wrong and really do what is right, apart from Jesus. To my amazement, I discovered that the best single-word definition for righteousness (and I didn't discover this until after college) is "Jesus"! Jesus is righteousness. He's the only One who has ever lived in this world who was righteous, and everyone else is unrighteous. "As it is written, There is none righteous, no, not one" (Romans 3:10). What does Paul say? How many righteous are there? None! "But," you say, "I'm a good liver." That may be true, but you are not righteous.

Therefore, if I want to have any kind of righteousness that is real, I must have Jesus. When I have Jesus, I have righteousness. There's no such thing as righteousness apart from

Jesus. "But," we say, "we know good people in the world who are kind and sweet, who do nice things." Yes, but those nice things have no heavenly value apart from a vital relationship with God. Apart from God, even nice things add to the sum of our sinfulness.

The third class I slept through was the one on faith. I thought that faith was making myself believe something and that if I didn't feel I had much faith, I should spend a lot of time working on my faith. I had the idea that if I could make myself believe something hard enough, it would happen. And the only problem with things not happening would be my lack of faith. Faith was something that you work up, and you work at, going through mental gymnastics to make yourself believe. After all, Jesus said, if you believe, all things are possible (see Mark 9:23). That's the only condition. So we work hard at believing and building up our faith.

Dr. Hutchins of the University of Chicago, in his satire on the Christian religion, pointed out that if you will center your positive thinking and your believing in the center cartoon of the Sunday comics, you can get just as many results as centering them on God. You can focus your belief on the center post in your backyard fence and accomplish just as much. And that's true if faith is nothing more than working up some kind of self-generated positive thinking. Whether you're trying to make yourself believe promises in God's Word or not, if you have to work on your faith, you have the wrong theology of faith. I slept through that class, and at one point it nearly destroyed me.

The Bible promise is that the greatest definition of faith is trust. And trust comes from knowing someone who's trustworthy. If you want to have genuine trust, you get acquainted with Jesus, and faith comes as a natural byproduct. You don't work it up; you don't work at it at all. Faith doesn't come to those who seek it; it comes to those who seek Jesus. It's the same way that righteousness comes. We don't become righteous by trying to do what's right. We become righteous by seeking Jesus and His righteousness.

Heavy classes! How can we sleep through them? If we sleep

through them, it leads to futile, frantic, pointless effort, endless work that gets us nowhere.

The fourth class I slept through was the one on Christianity. What is a Christian? I thought a Christian was a person who does what is right. So I was a Christian because I was doing what is right. But there are people in the world who do what is right who are not Christians. Haven't you seen people who do what is right, but couldn't care less about Jesus Christ? Aren't there people who will give the shirt off their back, who are kind, sweet, and honest, yet have nothing to do with Christianity? I've met them. There are all kinds of ethical, moral people in the world who would blaspheme the name of Jesus at any opportunity.

What is a Christian? I don't know where I was when they defined it in college. I'm sure somebody must have explained it. How can you know for sure that you are a real follower of Christ? There are two criteria: of whom do you love to talk and of whom do you love to think?

The disciples were first called Christians in Antioch, according to Acts 11. Why do you suppose they were called Christians? Because that's all they could talk about. Christ said this and Christ said that, and Christ did this and Christ did that. Finally the people said, "All these people can talk about is Christ. Why don't we call them *Christ*ians?" What would you be called today if you were called by what you talk about most of the time? What kind of words would be labels for you and for me?

The fifth class I slept through was the class on surrender. I thought that surrender was giving up the bad things that I was doing. And, of course, I didn't have that many, just a few, because of the proper training and background. But I did try to give up the few bad things I was doing.

If you are a strong person, you can succeed at this kind of surrender because strong people can succeed outwardly. So we would give up our tempers, we would give up listening to the wrong music, and we would give up eating between meals. Whatever was thought to be bad was set aside.

I had a friend who took all of his rock records—in those

days it was jazz—went out on a cliff, and played jazz frisbee. He said it was actually fun to see how far he could toss those records and listen to them go crashing down below. Beautiful! Righteousness by frisbee!

Getting rid of sins, giving up things, coming up to a higher standard—that's the usual idea about surrender. That's the class I slept through. Surrendering by giving up things? That's not surrender at all. Study it, and you will find that surrender has to do with giving up self. It is giving up on ourselves. It is giving up the idea that we can do anything at all within our hearts that counts, apart from Christ. All we can do is toss records. Inside, we still love them. Yes, strong people can deal with the externals. And an external religion has a great appeal to the multitudes.

I was doing pretty well on things, so I didn't need Jesus like my roommate did. He came from a tough background. His mother was killed by his father when he was four years old. He was tossed around from pillar to post as a child. He lied about his age and joined the navy, volunteering for suicide missions during the war. When he came back, he joined the police force and experienced many tough situations. So, of course, he needed Jesus. He had seen a lot of life. He spent hour after hour reading his Bible and praying. But, of course, I didn't need to. I was a good liver. I had given up all my bad things. I slept through that class on surrender, even though I had a roommate who had it straight.

Eventually, I discovered that surrender is coming to the place where you realize that nothing you can do really counts within, except coming to Jesus. John 15:5 says that without Jesus I can do nothing. Put that with Philippians 4:13, which says that with Him I can do all things. It leaves only one thing that we can possibly do in the realm of the deeper life—come to Jesus and keep coming to Jesus. He takes the initiative in that, but we must respond.

The sixth class I slept through was the one on the devotional life. Who needs a devotional life when you're getting along OK? Who needs a devotional life when you define sin in terms of doing bad things, and you're not doing that many

91

bad things? Who needs a devotional life when righteousness is doing what's right, and you've been doing what's right all your life? You were trained to righteousness by habit. Who needs a devotional life when you think that a Christian is someone who is a good liver, and you're doing pretty good? Who needs a devotional life when you've surrendered all these things and you've tricked yourself into thinking that all is right between you and God, on the basis of your behavior and your performance?

I'd like to remind you that one big reason why most professed Christians don't have a devotional life is that they still think they can live life independent of God and make it all right. No one really goes to his knees on his face before God until he comes to the end of his own resources and discovers his Best Friend. And the sooner you get there, my friend, the better.

So if you find yourself going under, and life is too much, stand up and sing the doxology. Go to your knees and say, "Thank *You*, Lord, for bringing me to the place where I can turn my life over to *You*."

I didn't realize that nine dollars with God's blessing is worth far more than ten dollars without His blessing 'till I tried it. But there's something more. Seven hours of sleep with God's blessing is worth far more than eight hours without it. Do you follow?

I didn't know that the devotional life was the entire basis of the Christian experience and the acceptance of Christ's righteousness, because His righteousness must be received on a daily basis. I didn't understand that when I was in college.

The last class I slept through, that I know about, was that Jesus loves to have people come to Him just as they are. I thought that if people came to Jesus, they would have to come after patching up their lives and changing their ways. I thought that you have to fix yourself up first in order to come to Jesus.

It finally dawned on me, the big breakthrough, the waking up out of sleep. We come to Jesus just as we are. I don't care who you are, how many failures, how many sins, how messed up your life is, if you will come to Jesus, He will accept you just as you are. He does the changing in your life because you can't. And He will bring you to the highest standard of living you have ever known, because the righteousness of Christ is not a cloak to cover unconfessed and unforsaken sins. It is a principle of life that transforms the character and controls the conduct.

And now, knowing the times, my friend, it is high time that we awake from our sleep.

An Eleventh-Hour Wake-up Call to God's Sleeping Army

A storm is coming. But despite the sound of distant thunder, most don't know what's ahead.

In *The Crisis of the End Time*, Marvin Moore suggests that history's climax is about to break upon us with startling speed and ferocity. He also shows how we can keep our relationship with Jesus during earth's darkest hour.

The Crisis is a forceful yet easy-to-understand explanation of the vital issues facing our church and our world on the eve of Christ's return.

US$10.95/Cdn$13.50. Paper.

THE **Crisis** OF THE **End Time**

Marvin Moore

To order, call TOLL FREE **1-800-765-6955** (in the U.S.), or visit your local ABC.

Prices subject to change without notice.

"I KNOW CHRIST HAS SAVED ME. SO WHY DO I STILL FEEL LOST?"

Ever feel like this? Do you worry over the "flatness" of your feelings in church, during prayer, or when you read the Bible?

In *Being Saved When You're Feeling Lost*, Dan Day reinforces the facts about our salvation and teaches simple skills in dealing with our often fickle emotions. Day's refreshing book provides a realistic view of feelings in the Christian life. In its pages you'll find real help in achieving a spiritual security you never thought possible.

US$8.95/Cdn$10.75. Paper.

Available now at your local ABC, or simply order by phone! Call TOLL FREE:
1-800-765-6955 (in the U.S.).

Prices subject to change without notice.

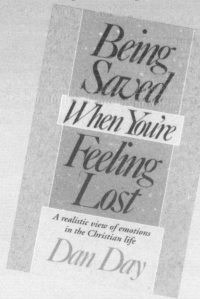